Life is Like a Taxi Ride

LIFE IS LIKE A TAXI RIDE

THE COLLECTED WISDOM
OF AN ECLECTIC BUSINESSMAN

Collected by

J. Lyman MacInnis, F.C.A., LLD.(Hon.)

HarperCollins*PublishersLtd*

http://www.harpercollins.com/canada

First edition

Canadian Cataloguing in Publication Data

MacInnis, J. Lyman, 1938–
    Life is like a taxi ride : the collected wisdom of an eclectic businessman

ISBN 0-00-255750-9

1. Success. I. Title.

BF637.S8M135 1997   158   C97-931236-1

---

97 98 99 ❖ HC 10 9 8 7 6 5 4 3 2 1

Printed and bound in the United States

Contents

Acknowledgements

I'VE HAD ABOUT A DOZEN secretaries during the forty years I've been working on this collection, and many of them have had to type, re-type and re-classify thousands of entries — a daunting and, I'm sure, boring task in the pre-computer years. Three of them deserve special mention. They are Darlene Mantini, Joan Schultz and Kathryn Evelyn.

At HarperCollins, Judy Brunsek has long believed in the merit of this project, and she, Don Loney, Iris Tupholme and Claude Primeau have conspired wonderfully to make it happen.

My wife, Anne, and sons, Matthew and Alan, are probably sick to death of most of these "wisdoms," but they continue to support and humour me.

I thank you all.

Introduction

THERE ARE FEW, if any, original "wisdoms" in this book. Goethe said, "Everything has been thought of before; the trick is to think of it again." And somebody else observed that "there is nothing new under the sun." What *is* original, though, is the way in which these "wisdoms" have been interpreted and expressed herein. These interpretations reflect my views of the world we occupy, the people we share it with, and what goes on around us.

I don't know exactly when I began collecting the "wisdoms," but it was 1957 when I started to write them down. Whenever I read, heard, saw or otherwise experienced anything that taught me something, I jotted down, at the first opportunity, my interpretation of whatever that was. And, forty years later, I still manage to pick up one every now and then.

Some of the "wisdoms," particularly the very short

observations, may be expressed verbatim, in the way I first read or heard them, but I doubt it. If it turns out that I have directly quoted anyone's original material, it is certainly inadvertent; but if such is the case, please send proof thereof to the publishers and we will appropriately deal with the situation in future editions of the collection.

Ability

As a very young boy, I idolized him. He had so much ability! He was a good baseball player, and a great hockey player. He even played football well, which practically no one else in our little town did. On top of his athletic ability, he could sing and play the guitar. He was also a gifted graphic artist. And, believe it or not, he always had the highest marks in his class. The only question, it seemed, was in which of the various fields open to him would he become a huge success. Regrettably, the answer was "none." You see, he never *used* any of his myriad of abilities. He dropped out of high school, drifted from menial job to menial job, became an alcoholic, and died far too young.

When *you* aren't improving, someone else is; and when you compete with that person, you will lose.

The greatest ability is *depend*ability.

Know what you *can't* do as well as what you *can* do.

Talent is worth only what you do with it.
A Ripley cartoon showed a bar of iron worth $5.
Made into horseshoes, it would be worth $10.
Made into needles, $3,285. If made into balance springs
for watches, its worth would be $250,000.

Natural ability without education
beats education without natural ability.

Hard work without ability is a shame;
ability without hard work is a tragedy.

Rarer than ability is the ability to recognize ability.

Necessity develops ability.

The more ability people have,
the easier their jobs look.

If you can't dance,
don't set your heart on the prom.

You needn't be sick to get better.

Advice

Two DOWN-AT-THE-HEEL OLD BOYS were sitting propped against a large shipping crate on the pier, watching a luxury yacht go by. The people on board were obviously having a great time.

"You know," said one, "the reason I'm in here and not out there on that yacht is that I *never* listened to *any* advice from *anybody*."

"That's funny," replied the other, "the reason *I'm* not out there on that yacht is that I *always* listened to *all* advice from *everybody*."

Always listen to advice, but don't necessarily follow it.

People willingly accept advice if it doesn't interfere
with what they want to do.

There's a lot of difference between advice and help.

There are three times when we should never give advice to people: when they are tired, when they are angry, and when they have just made a mistake.

Ask enough people, and you'll find somebody to tell you to do what you were going to do anyway.

You often don't know whether advice is good or bad until it's no longer needed.

People who like advice the least are those who need it the most. That's why.

There's no point giving good advice if you set a bad example.

People wouldn't ask for help if they thought they could handle the problem themselves. But when they ask for advice, they might just want to talk.

Ask questions. If you don't understand the problem, people aren't going to listen to your advice.

Good advice doesn't come in one-size-fits-all.

Ageing

THE BOY BROUGHT AN ACORN into the kitchen and asked his eighty-year-old grandfather what it was. His grandfather explained that it was really a big seed, and if they planted it in the backyard the boy's grandchildren would eventually be able to climb the great oak that would grow from it.

"But, it'll take years and years," complained the boy.

"Yup," said Grandfather, getting up from his chair, "so we'd better go out and plant it right now."

Old age is when we know all the answers
but nobody asks any questions.

Middle age is when the telephone rings on a
Saturday night and you hope it's not for you.

You're getting old when the candles
cost more than the cake.

Growing old is fine, considering the alternative.

We all want a long life but not old age.

The older we get, the better we were.

At my age I don't need to be informed,
just reminded.

Never retire from life, regardless of your age.

Your real age is how old you feel right after you've
tried to show someone how young you feel.

The old know more about being young than
the young know about being old.

The young learn. The old understand.

You're never as old as you're going to be.

I'm not as good as I once was,
but I'm as good once as I ever was.

I can still jump as high, I just can't stay up as long.

I'm as good as I ever was—
there are just fewer opportunities to prove it.

If you're still alive, there are still things to be done.

We are as young as our dreams
and as old as our doubts.

People who think they're too old to try something new
probably always were.

We need imaginative and doubting youth to turn
things upside down. But we also need old fogies to
prevent youth from turning upside down things
that should stay right side up.

You're only young once,
but you can be immature indefinitely.

We're not old until regrets replace dreams.

When growth stops, decay begins.

The young know the rules, but old-timers
know the exceptions.

Anger

SHE WAS THE BEST TEACHER I ever had. And I had made her
angry. I knew there was punishment in store, but she just
sat there and stared at me.

"Well," I finally mustered enough nerve to ask, "what's
going to happen to me?"

"I can't decide right now," she replied. "I'll have to
wait until I get over being mad at you."

He who strikes first admits he has no more ideas.

People are as big as the things that make them angry.

He who loses his head is usually the last to miss it.

Those who truly know don't need to shout.

The angriest people are those who know they are wrong.

Your temper is one of your most valuable possessions.
Don't lose it.

When right, we can afford to keep our tempers.
When wrong, we can't afford to lose them.

It may take years to build a relationship,
but a single angry act can destroy one.

Never forget what people say when they are angry.

What you say when you're angry
may be the best speech you'll ever regret.

Get as angry as you want to, but vent it in private.

When angry, count to ten before you speak;
when very angry, count to one hundred.

Anger is only one letter short of danger.

Anger is frequently caused
by having no one to blame but yourself.

Hot heads and cold hearts can't solve anything.

It's easy to be angry. But few people have the ability
to be angry with the right person, for the right reason,
to the right degree, at the right time, in the right way.

Anger harms the vessel in which it is held more
than anything on which it is poured.

If someone makes you angry, they've conquered you.

You can't save face by losing your head.

Anger may get us into trouble,
but it's usually pride that keeps us there.

Before getting angry,
ask yourself if this will matter in a year.

The one who loses his temper has the problem—not you.

It's always more effective to support your argument
than to raise your voice.

Angry words usually indicate a weak argument.

One problem with fighting fire with fire
is that you end up with a lot of ashes.

When the other person gets angry,
end the argument.

On both the road and in an argument,
seeing red means it's time to stop.

Angry people usually don't cool down
until they blow off their head of steam.
Only after you let them should you try
to reason with them.

Before giving someone a piece of your mind,
be sure you'll have enough left.

Arguments

THERE IS A SONG (we've long since forgotten the name of it), but there is a lyric in it that says "do what you do do well." For almost forty years now, the three of us have been arguing about what that lyric means. One of us insists it means that you should do *only* what you do well. Another insists it means that *whatever* you do, you should do it well. The third says that if you follow either of the other two suggestions you will achieve both, so therefore, it means both.

Don't argue with people
whose opinions you don't respect.

You can't reason people out of something
they weren't reasoned into.

It is better to debate an issue without settling it
than to settle it without debating it.

A long, drawn-out argument is a sign neither side is right.

Arguments for and against vary in importance
with one's point of view.

The best argument is an effective explanation.

When someone says they agree in principle,
the argument is underway.

The best way to answer a bad argument is to let it go on.

It's awfully frustrating to argue with people
who know what they're talking about.

Ignorance causes a lot of interesting arguments.

The best way to get the last word is to apologize.

There are two sides to every argument;
there are also two sides to every sheet of flypaper,
but it makes a big difference to the fly which side he's on.

Everyone has a right to an opinion,
but no one has a right to be wrong about facts.

Arguing isn't the best way to show that a stick is crooked;
just lay a straight stick beside it.

Remember, "yes, but ..." *is* an argument.

Arguments always interrupt discussions.

To prevent an argument's recurrence,
find and correct its cause.

Letting someone have their own way is often the best way
to prove them wrong.

It's annoying to find someone arguing on your side that
you wish was on the other side.

Only your neighbours listen to both sides of an argument.

An argument always has two sides. It needs an end.

It takes two to start an argument,
but one can end it.

Disagreement over an issue shouldn't cause disagreement
between people. Always separate the issue
from the personality.

The best way to win an argument is to be right.

Win all your arguments, lose all your friends.

When we understand the other person's viewpoint,
usually he is trying to do right.

Hard arguments require soft words.

Everybody doesn't want the same thing,
so everybody isn't persuaded by the same arguments.

Time makes more converts than reasons.

Trying to change people's viewpoints
when they're worked up about something
will only make them harden their positions.

More minds are changed through observation
than through argument.

Attitude

THERE IS A TRIANGLE OF SUCCESS. The left side is knowledge. But, we all know knowledgeable people who have failed. The right side of the triangle of success represents skills with which to apply knowledge. But, we also know knowledgeable and skilled people who have failed. Those are the ones who don't possess the base of the triangle, which is "attitude."

You see, our attitude is the only factor in life over which we have complete control. No one can change it or affect it unless we let them. I once asked a very successful, and always happy, colleague what the secrets of his success and happiness were. He replied, "Every day when I get up, I pretend there's a bucket of characteristics at the side of my bed, any one of which I can choose to wear for the day. I always pick a positive attitude."

_____

The only thing in life over which we have complete control
is our mental attitude.

If it's to be, it's up to me.

Things work out best for people
who make the best of things.

We're not born with our attitudes—we develop them.

To change your world, change your thoughts.

Consider these three A's of life: ability, ambition and attitude. Ability earns you your pay cheque. Ambition gets
you raises. Attitude determines the amount of both.

Some things have to be believed to be seen.

If you don't know you can't do something, you'll do it.

To be absolutely certain about something,
you must know everything or nothing about it.

Not to know is bad; not wanting to know is terrible.

If you've decided that you can't do it,
you're probably right.

We become like we think.

Whether life grinds us down or polishes us up
depends on us.

It's expectations that cause frustration.

Talent determines what you *can* do,
motivation what you *do* do, and attitude what you *will* do.

You may not be able to control circumstances or people,
but you *can* control your attitude toward them.

Love of flowers won't make you a good gardener;
you must also hate weeds.

Don't judge a day by the weather.

To discover the best in yourself,
look for the good in others.

You don't have to like facts in order to face them.

Somebody's opinion doesn't make something a fact.

Bad weather always looks worse when you're inside looking out. Go out into it, get wet, and it's not so bad.

Until you realize your strengths, you don't have any.

Easy tasks become hard when done reluctantly.

The mind is like a clock,
it has to be wound up with good thoughts.

When you say, "I can't do that" add the word "*yet.*"

When it's over, let it go. If you can't put it down gently,
don't pick it up.

When your goal seems far away,
consider a sculptor chipping at a rock a hundred times
without a crack showing. Then the next blow splits it.
It wasn't the 101st blow that did it, but the 101st
and all the others.

I'd rather be looked over than overlooked.

No matter how tough things get,
you'll do better with a cheerful approach.

Whatever you're going through,
it probably isn't as serious as you think.

In times like these, it's good to recall
there have always been times like these.

Life is ten percent what you make it
and ninety percent how you take it.

Whether you think you can or can't do something,
you're probably right.

If you can't have what you like,
try liking what you have.

Behaviour

ANNE AND I WERE GOING to a cocktail party that I didn't particularly want to attend. Just before we rang the doorbell, she put her hand on my arm and said, "Lyman, if it's dull — leave it that way!"

Think like a person of action, act like a person of thought.

We are more efficient
when we forget what is unimportant.

We don't get a second chance to make a first impression.

If you don't want people to know about it, don't do it.

Ducks are calm and unruffled on the surface,
but they're paddling furiously underneath.

Earn one more tomorrow by what you do today.

Add a little to a little and do it often.
Soon the little thing will be a big thing.

No matter how soft and warm your bed
you still have to get out of it.

Your exercise program shouldn't include running down
your friends, jumping to conclusions,
or side-stepping responsibility.

Dress just a *little* better than the occasion calls for.

We have to keep busy in order to manage
our physical and mental energy.

Study hard, think quietly, talk gently, act frankly:
You'll win out in the long run.

If you don't conquer self, you'll be conquered by self.

An appeaser feeds a crocodile hoping it will eat him last.

The steps don't change from childhood. We learn to roll over, then sit up, then crawl, then walk and, finally, run.

Without involvement there's rarely commitment.

Be pleasant until ten o'clock in the morning and the rest of the day will take care of itself.

Be effective with people, efficient with things.

It's tough to talk yourself out of something you behaved yourself into.

Build strengths; delegate weaknesses.

Differentiate between stability and paralysis.

Always try to make yourself more useful.

Taking a stand on something that matters is a proud and satisfying moment.

Don't crawl when you feel like running.

Whenever someone else's opinion of you counts, be at your very best.

Improving what you have is better than wishing
for what you don't have.

You can't row a boat in two different directions
at the same time.

Sometimes it's better to let nature take its course
than to adhere to hard, fast goals.

If an activity adds to your life,
continue it. If it doesn't, stop it.

Be a mentor, not a tormentor.

Use what you have and develop what you don't.

To *be*come, *over*come.

A sure way to get out of a rut is to give something
unexpected to someone who doesn't expect it.

Want to check on just how different people are?
Buy two copies of the same book. Give one to someone
whom you feel thinks most like you. Read one yourself.
Both of you underline any *new points* the book brought
out. Then compare your underlinings.

A lady is a woman in whose presence I'm inspired
to act as a gentleman.

Loneliness is negative—solitude is positive.
Be able to be alone.

Nothing can bother you unless you let it.

In addition to doing the right things
you have to do things right.

To really know a person, observe his behaviour
when he thinks no one is watching.

People who take a stand are *sometimes* wrong;
people who never take a stand are *always* wrong.

Think of how others should be,
then start being like that yourself.

When wrong, be willing to change;
when right, be easy to live with.

When things go wrong, imagine that your best friend is the
other person involved. Then start dealing with the person
as you would your best friend,
regardless of what you may have to do later.

Confronting the strong is admirable;
bullying the weak is not.

Don't make a big wave out of a little ripple.

Work harder to be respected than to be loved.

Don't dwell on minor aches or small disappointments.

When someone else blows your horn,
the sound carries farther.

People can't see eye to eye with you
when you're looking down on them.

Bores and Boredom

IT WAS A MIND-NUMBING JOB for a fifteen-year-old. For eight hours a day, five days a week, I had to sort pieces of paper, identified by six-digit numbers, into their numerical sequence. To survive, I began to work out ways to make the job more challenging. For example, I would imagine each new piece of paper as a sports statistic, such as goals, assists and penalty minutes, or hits, runs and errors, pretending that each one represented one of my seasons in the big leagues. Another tactic was to estimate how many sheets were in a handful, sort them, and see how close my estimate was. Given some thought, there were many ways to beat the boredom.

Bored people are usually boring.

Bores take away solitude without providing company.

To deal with a boring situation, improve it.

Only one person can solve all the world's problems,
and it's amazing how often you get to sit beside him.

Imagination is a wonderful cure for boredom.

People with the gift of gab often don't know
how to wrap it up.

There are basically two kinds of boring people:
those who never speak up, and those who never shut up.

If you're intelligent, and you're bored, it's your fault.

People always prefer to be inspired than to be bored.

Being boring is often a sign
of not being too sure of yourself.

No job should be boring because there's always
the challenge of how it can be done better.

There is no such thing as a boring subject.
But there *are* disinterested people.
To become interested in something, learn more about it.

Nothing is interesting if we're not interested.
Get interested, and stay interested.
Find the thrill; then enjoy it.

Bureaucracy

A LOW-LEVEL CIVIL SERVANT mistakenly read a highly confidential document. After reading the document, and before passing it on to the next person on the list, he placed his initials beside his name. When his superiors found out that he had been mistakenly included on the restricted circulation list, he was asked to erase his initials and initial the erasure.

Bureaucracy is when the person who answers the phone can't help you.

Bureaucracy at its worst is better
than bureaucracy at its best.

Change

REMEMBER A SERIES OF ADVERTISEMENTS a few years ago in which men with black eyes were depicted along with the line that they would "rather fight than switch"? Well, folks, that's the way it is in real life. Most people would rather fight than change. Asking people to change anything is like asking them to throw away a pair of comfortable, old slippers.

To understand how hard it is to change others,
consider how hard it is to change yourself.

People support things they help create.

Understanding them—not bullying or tricking them—is
the key to getting people to change.

When someone suggests a new way to do something,
instead of considering why it might not work,
look for one reason why it might.

If people don't care about a problem,
they won't care about the solution.

When dealing with things that are wrong,
don't change things that are right.

Asking "which" rather than "if" provides a choice
between one thing or another,
not between something and nothing.

Before deciding on a change,
get the views of those who will be most affected by it.
They are usually the best source for improvements.

Most people prefer old problems to new solutions.

You can't always make people like change, but
you can find ways to make them feel less threatened by it.

To get people to accept change,
convince them now they'll be better off.

People are less likely to resist change when they know
exactly what lies ahead. Strategies worked on collectively
have a better chance of being accepted.

Change in response to success is a lot easier
than change in response to failure.

Not everything that we face can be changed,
but nothing can be changed until it *is* faced.

Expect change, except possibly from the pop machine.

Most changes are accomplished with compromise.

We can't improve everything all at once. But
often a little change now will result in a big change later.

When trying to implement change,
remember that somebody is responsible for the status quo,
and it might be the person you're talking to.

Successful changes come from doing
as little damage as possible.

Remember that old ways may be old for a reason.

The best way to change someone is to treat them
the way they could be, not the way they are.

Evolution is preferable to revolution.

Hold onto old ways of doing things as long as they are good,
then accept new ways when they are better.

You can't influence a person you don't understand.

To change an attitude, find out what causes it.

Tell people a thousand times they can do something
and they still may not believe you.
Show them once and they'll be convinced.

Character

I WAS YOUNG, probably eighteen or so, the winter day that Brian and I were driving down a slippery hill in an isolated area just east of Toronto. Brian was a relatively new driver with a relatively old car. We were inching along when he lost control and skidded into a parked car. Brian's bumper hit the door of the other car. There was no damage at all to Brian's car, but the door on the driver's side of the other car was pretty well crunched.

The car we hit was the only other one within sight, and there wasn't a person to be seen anywhere. There were no houses close enough for anyone to be able to see the license numbers. Even so, Brian left a note with his name, address and telephone number on it.

What you don't have inside can't been seen on the outside.

Humility is like underwear. Have it, but don't show it.

Personality can open doors,
but only character can keep them open.

In matters of principle, stand like a rock;
in matters of taste, swim with the current.

It's what we are that comes through,
not what we're trying to be.

What you are may speak so loudly
that people can't hear what you say.

When we pray, let's ask for a change in character
rather than a change in circumstances.

The books people read
will tell you a great deal about them.

It's not *who* you know that counts —
it's how you are known by those who know *you*.

The measure of a man's real character
is what he would do if he knew he would
never be found out.

People reveal their character by their reaction to jokes.

Brains and experience can be bought,
but character is something a person must supply himself.

Character is what you are in the dark.

Character is developed by *earning* things,
not by getting them for nothing.

Character is much easier kept than recovered.

Be more concerned about your character
than about your reputation. Character is what you *really* are.
Reputation is just what other people *think* you are.

Character is a by-product produced by
what you do consistently.

Reaction to temptation reveals character.

Adversity can be a test of character,
but to *really* test character, give a person power.

If you're going to insist on your rights,
be prepared to live up to your responsibilities.

Insulting remarks about you are meaningless
if you live so that nobody will believe them.

To live a worthwhile life, decide
what you want written on your tombstone.

A good measure of a person's character
is how he behaves when wrong.

Reputation ultimately reflects reality.

Credibility is hard to get but easy to lose.

Character includes having both self-respect
and respect for others.

The difference between character and behaviour is that
behaviour may work in one situation but not another.
Character always works. Behaviour is specific;
character is fundamental.

Character is power.

We will ultimately be judged on what we *really* are,
not on what we *appear* to be.

The right motive is more important than the right move.

Judge people by their questions as well as their answers.

Character isn't what you say you believe —
it's the way you live.

People are also known by the company they keep clear of.

People are judged by what they stand in line for.

Character is best measured by consideration
and tolerance for others.

Don't let others set your standards.

It's fine to stand on principles
as long as you don't fall down on duties.

Thoughts put into words turned into actions become
habits which build character and determine our destiny.

Better to be faithful than famous.

Money will buy a good dog,
but it won't buy the wag of his tail.

Charity

AFTER I SAW HIM GIVE what I thought was a very generous amount of money, I complimented him on his charitable nature. "That's not charity," he corrected me. "I can afford it."

Charity may begin at home — but it shouldn't end there.

Generosity is not measured by how much you give,
but by how much you have left.

When you give, forget; when you receive, remember.

We make a living from what we get;
we make our lives from what we give.

Children

"I DON'T KNOW WHY you let the kids play ball hockey in your backyard every year," said the crusty visitor. "It ruins your grass."

My father replied, "The grass will always be there; the kids won't."

Parents who don't discipline their children
refer to their cop-out as child psychology.

You can accomplish most things with children
if you play with them.

Children who live with approval,
learn to live with themselves.

Children need love most of all when they don't deserve it.

Spend half as much money and twice as much time
raising your children.

In raising your children *presence* is more important
than *presents*.

Our best legacy is well-educated children.

Find out what your children want to do,
and if it's reasonable, then teach them
the best way to do it.

Children need supporters more than they need critics.

By the time we realize *our* parents were right,
our children think *we're* wrong.

The family you come from isn't as important
as the family you're going to have.

Love your children unconditionally.
You have them for a very short time.

Time spent with your children is never wasted.

Teenagers need to be reminded
that eventually they will be as stupid as their parents.

The two most important things parents
can give their children are roots and wings.

There'd be a lot less problems with children
if they had to shovel manure to keep the TV running.

Small boys become big men by being in the company of
big men who care about small boys.

What you say to your kids will be heard by posterity.

A good parent remembers what is was like to be a kid.

Drive as if *your* kids were in the other car.

Whenever you have to do something new or difficult,
ask yourself how you would do it if your kids
were watching, then do it accordingly.

Parents know a lot more about being fifteen than their
children know about being fifty.

Communication

I WAS PLAYING GOAL in a charity hockey game, the proceeds of which were going to help a young man who had sustained a brain injury such that he would never play hockey again. But on this special night he was dressed in his hockey gear and he was going to take a penalty shot on me. The referee told me that the player had been instructed to "go left." Of course, I was to let him score, so when he skated right in on my goal, I "went right." Only when it was obvious that I'd made a great stop on the "penalty shot" did we all realize that his "left" was my "right."

Folks like to deal with people who make them feel good.

If you want people to pay attention,
tell them it's confidential.
Some people will believe anything that's whispered.

People become what you encourage them to be,
not what you nag them to be.

The best way to get clear answers is to ask clear questions.

Answers that sound good
aren't necessarily good, sound answers.

One specific is worth a thousand generalities.

Anything than *can* be misunderstood
will be misunderstood.

To succeed in communicating,
say it like it's never been said before.

To get action, appeal to emotions.
To appeal to emotions, get emotional.

After you learn the language
you then have to learn what you're talking about.

All communication is a form of selling.
So think about this. If a salesperson can't sell something,
is it the customer's fault?

Lightning is more impressive than thunder.

Mean what you say. Say what you mean.
But, don't say it mean.

Don't change your style for different audiences.
Be basically the same whether you're giving a speech,
engaged in a conversation, or being interviewed by the
media. Don't change because the situation changes.

Make points, not enemies.

People don't want to hear about the labour pains —
they want to see the baby.

Speaking or writing without thinking
is like shooting without aiming.

Effective communication doesn't ensure success,
but poor communication certainly contributes to failure.

A teacher walked into a rambunctious classroom,
slapped her hand on her desk and shouted,
"I want pandemonium!"
The students quieted down immediately.
It sometimes isn't what you demand that's important
as much as the way you demand it.

Conversation

HE WAS STANDING OFF all by himself at the cocktail party. There were a few people I knew there, but I decided I could talk to them later. I went over to him and asked, "Do you have the same trouble as I do in starting up a conversation?"

He replied, "I'm sure my problem is much worse."

My next question was, "Why do you think this is?"

Fifteen minutes later, we were still talking about how hard it was for strangers to strike up a conversation.

Wit is the salt of conversation, not the food.

Most people never make a long story short
until it's too late.

Many people have very little to say,
but we have to listen a long time to find out.

Be sure your conversation isn't a monologue
delivered in front of a witness.

To encourage conversation between two
people at a meeting, seat them face to face;
to discourage confrontation, sit them side by side.

One way to learn a bit about someone is to ask him to
describe the worst day he ever had and how he handled it.

Ask questions in a friendly tone of voice.
You're more apt to get the answer you want.

Consider even hostile questions
as simply requests for information.

There's no need to shout if the right words are used.

Think of your clever remark in time to say it —
or not say it — as the case might be.

The best question in any conversation is "why?"

When someone says, "I'll think it over and let you know,"
you already know.

When receiving a complaint,
assume at the beginning that it's legitimate.

Most of the friction of daily life
is caused by the wrong tone of voice.

How you say something may determine the response.

A good conversationalist asks
the questions you want to answer.

Be genuinely interested in others.

It's better to ask some of the questions
than to know all the answers.

Always sacrifice a clever retort
for the sake of someone's feelings.

Don't make a statement when you can ask a question.

The tongue is usually wet, therefore prone to slip.

Always say less than you think.

Engage brain before starting tongue.

Co-operation

ONE OF THE BEST EXAMPLES of the effectiveness of co-operation is the traffic light. When we all co-operate at the intersection by adhering to the signals, chaos is avoided. When we don't, people sometimes get killed.

You haven't used all your strength until you ask for help.

There's almost no limit to what can be done
if it doesn't matter who gets the credit.

The biggest step you can take is the one you take
when you meet the other person halfway.

It's better to give than to lend. The recipient thinks more
of you and the cost is usually the same.

Don't be a threat, be essential.

Bolster others' weaknesses with your strengths.

Don't take over tasks that other people enjoy.

The greatest help you can give
is to help someone help himself.

If we all swept in front of our own door,
the whole town would be clean.

To succeed you have to be as ready to accept
other people's ideas as you are your own.

Competition in the marketplace
requires co-operation in the workplace.

A candle loses nothing by lighting another candle.

Which is the most important leg of a three-legged stool?

Many united spider webs can trap a large animal.

We aren't here to see through one another,
but to see one another through.

If you can't help, at least don't hurt.

By helping a person up a hill you get to the top yourself.

Give someone a boost when they need it
and you will be fondly remembered.

To get what *you* want,
help lots of people get what *they* want.

Spelling lessons: Co-operation can be spelled
with two letters — we; and, there's no "I" in *team*.

People co-operate
when they feel they are part of the decision.

To eliminate rivalries,
give people joint goals they can reach together.

Courage

MY COUSIN PATRICIA was born with spina bifida. The prognosis, of course, was that she would be so severely handicapped that a normal life was out of the question. Well, she does lead a normal life. She walks, she drives, she plays catch, she teaches school. Yes, medical advances and a seemingly endless series of operations contributed. Yes, the tremendous support and encouragement of a loving family contributed. But the most important contributing factor was, and is, Patricia's courage. It may have faltered at times, but it never failed. Her courage continues to be an inspiration to all of us who are lucky enough to know her.

It takes courage to be able to let go of the familiar.

Courage, like muscles, is strengthened by use.

Courage is the quality that guarantees all others.

Courage is being scared to death of something —
but facing it anyway.

Courage can't be judged because
it's impossible to tell how frightened someone is.

Courage is fear that has said its prayers.

Rather than praying for an obstacle to be removed,
pray for the courage to overcome it.

Leaders have the confidence to evaluate
and the courage to act.

Face issues at once, and face them squarely.

Criticism

I HAD NEVER READ a radio commercial, and yet here I was in a studio about to record five of them. I did the first one and the producer told me it was fine. I did the second one and the producer told me it was fine. And so on until all five were done. Then the producer said to me, "Let's do the first one over again." When he played it back for me it was obvious that the first take was terrible. When I asked him why he didn't have me re-do it right away, he replied, "Had I criticized the first one right after you'd done it, we'd be re-doing five of them now, not just one."

We shouldn't speak ill of predecessors —
we didn't walk in their shoes.

Criticism from a wise person beats praise from a fool.

It's fine to give people credit in writing,
but criticize them only in person.

Nothing equals the urge to edit someone else's draft.
Be sure you improve it, not just change it.

Don't mind criticism. If it's not justified,
you can ignore it; if it is justified, learn from it.

Criticize the fault, not the person.

Critics don't write plays, make movies,
paint pictures, or build things.

Most people would rather be ruined by praise
than saved by criticism.

Some opposition can help; kites rise against the wind,
not with it.

Superior people blame themselves;
the inferior blame others.

You learn from those who dispute things with you.

A critic knows the way but can't drive the car.

The only way to escape criticism is to do nothing,
say nothing and be nothing.

Most critics are like eunuchs. They know how it's done,
they see it done every day, but they can't do it themselves.

There is a time to wink as well as to see.

The time to deal with a justified criticism is immediately.

The people to worry about are not those who openly
criticize us, but those who disagree with us
and don't let us know.

Nothing deflates a critic quicker
than to accept the criticism in a grateful manner.

If it will hurt to criticize someone,
you'll probably do it right. If you're looking forward to it,
hold your tongue.

People shouldn't be criticized for making a mistake,
but they should be criticized if they don't learn from it.

When someone criticizes you,
remember he's probably just mad at himself.

There are no statues honouring critics.

Praising the good things people do
is more enjoyable than criticizing the bad.

Whatever decision you make,
someone will tell you you're wrong.
Remember that critics aren't always right.

Until you figure out how to criticize constructively,
keep quiet.

Never let anyone hear your criticism second-hand.

Criticism, properly given, helps people improve.

When criticizing, focus on the future.

Always discuss negatives in private.

The guy who won't lift a finger to help
is usually the first to point one.

The less we complain the more sympathy we get.

Look for faults with a mirror, not binoculars.

Avoid people who criticize your ambitions —
they're probably failures. Truly successful people
want you to be successful, too.

When being critical of yourself, use your head;
when being critical of others, use your heart.

The person who doesn't criticize when he should
is as wrong as the person who never praises.

Don't find fault, find a cure.

Before criticizing,
think about what alternative you're going to suggest.

You can't throw mud without getting dirty hands.

Cynicism

HE WAS THE CRANKIEST, most fault-finding person I've ever encountered, yet every morning when we all arrived for work Frank always went over to him and chatted for a few moments.

When I asked Frank if he was trying to change him, Frank replied, "Hell, no. No one will ever change him. I just want to start my day listening to him complain for a couple of minutes because from then on things will only get better."

A good portion of the population
is always against everything.

Cynics know the price of everything
and the value of nothing.

It's hard to believe that someone is telling the truth
when you know that you would lie in their circumstances.

Cynics try to make the world as miserable for us
as they make it for themselves.

A cynic is one of the crowning works of the devil.

Light a candle rather than curse the dark.

It's usually easier to hate something than to understand it.

Most people would rather suffer than think.

Never coddle a malcontent.

It's been said that misery loves company.
Actually, it *demands* it! Miserable people
want us to be miserable, too.

Cheerful people get sick less than cynics.

Most of the time cynics don't have much fun,
the rest of the time they don't have any at all.

Cynics lead a tough life.
They also cause the most grief for the rest of us.

Decision Making

THE YOUNG LAD from rural Prince Edward Island had gotten a well-paying job at the largest potato warehouse in Charlottetown. When he showed up at eight o'clock in the morning, the foreman took him to a remote area of the massive building where a pile of tens of thousands of potatoes stood beside a vacant area about the size of a football field. The foreman said, "All you have to do is sort that big pile into three piles: small, medium and large." At ten-thirty, when the foreman came to tell the boy he could take a break, he was surprised to see that the big pile was undisturbed and the empty area was still empty. Not one potato had been moved. There sat the boy, still holding in his hand the first potato he selected, saying, "I can't make up my mind which size it is."

Our decisions will be no better than our information.

There's a big difference between good,
sound reasons and reasons that sound good.

Everyone has a right to an opinion,
but no one has a right to be wrong about facts.

Most of us risk disaster rather than read directions.

Making up your mind is often like making up a bed;
it helps to have someone on the other side.

Opposition is often proof you're on the right track.

Avoid the two extremes — unwarranted delay on one
hand, and impulsive, snap decisions on the other.

When pressured into making a quick decision,
the best answer is always "no,"
because it's easier to change a *no* to a *yes* than vice versa.

Quick questions sometimes need slow answers.

Don't rush a decision if there's no reason to.

If action is urgently needed,
a poor decision may be better than no decision at all.
Any decision is usually better than none.

It's better to be right half of the time and get something
done than to get nothing done and never be wrong.

The person who must know the perfect result
before deciding, never decides.

Decision is a scalpel that cuts clean and straight;
indecision is a dull knife that leaves ragged gashes.

Any decision you have to sleep on
will probably keep you awake.

You can't sleep on something before making a decision
if your competition doesn't need the sleep.

Simple solutions may not be right,
but they should always be considered first.

It would be easier to make the right decisions
if second thoughts came first.

Never trade the long term for the short term.

Don't make a decision until your emotions are in neutral.

When gut feel and logic suggest the same decision,
you're definitely right.

When a decision is made, direct all your energy to making
it work.

State your decision, not your reason.
Your decision may be right
while your reason may be wrong.

You may not be able to control the results of a decision,
but you can control the process.

Eliminate options that would result
in outcomes you can't live with.

You have to practice making decisions.

Making decisions gets easier the more you do it.

We can control our choices
but often we can't control their consequences.
When we carry a board, we pick up both ends.

Before reacting, understand the cause
of whatever it is you're about to react to.

Indecision is the father of worry
and the mother of unhappiness.

Stay in the middle of the road too long
and you're apt to get run over.

The wiser the decision
the more apt it is to cause displeasure.

When you don't know what to do,
it may be best to do nothing.

Diplomacy and Tact

AS THE GUEST SPEAKER droned on endlessly, the bored head-table guest turned to the lady beside him and said, "I can't stand that man." She exclaimed, "That's my husband!" The bored head-table guest never missed a beat as he retorted, "That's why I can't stand him."

More enemies are made by what we say
than friends by what we do.

Make visitors feel at home,
even though you wish they were.

Pretend to learn things you already know.

To live happily with people,
overlook their faults and admire their good points.

Diplomacy is knowing how to do something and, without comment, watch somebody else doing it wrongly.

Know which bridge to cross and which bridge to burn.

When asked why she married Mark and not Larry, Susan replied, "When I was with Larry I thought *he* was the cleverest person in the world, but when I'm with Mark he makes *me* think I'm the cleverest person in the world."

Diplomacy is telling someone he has an open mind when you really believe he has a hole in his head.

Be wiser than people if you can. But don't let them know.

People, like bullets, go farthest when they are smoothest.

If you understand why prickly pears are prickly, you can allow for it.

It's possible to be honest and direct without being hurtful. But it does require some thought.

Sometimes the best way to convince people they're wrong is to let them have their own way.

See others as they wish to be seen.

Don't bother to talk about yourself.
Others will do that when you leave.

Save face for others and your face looks better, too.

Be nice to people on your way up,
because you're going to see them again on your way down.

Sticks and stones may break bones,
but words may break a heart.
You can always be honest without being brutal.

Talent knows *what* to do; tact knows *when* to do it.
Talent is something, but tact is everything.

Tact can build a fire under people
without making their blood boil.

If you scare people,
they'll be around only as long as they're scared.

Don't cut something that can be untied.

Patting a person on the back
is the best way to knock a chip off his shoulder.

Use your head to handle yourself,
and your heart to handle others.

Be sure that frank and candid
do not become tactless and cruel.

Be sure your tact isn't deceit.

Wise people are like rivers;
the deeper they are the less noise they make.

A real test of a diplomat is to have the same ailment
another person is describing and not mention it.

Mark Twain said that good breeding
consisted of concealing how much we think of ourselves
and how little we think of others.

Don't think with your mouth.

Differences of opinion should be settled right away.
Delay can destroy a relationship,
so give it your full attention immediately.

Dreams

I WORKED FOR SEVEN YEARS with one of the most brilliant, technical people in his particular field. He was always practical. He could solve the most difficult technical problems. But, the only time he seemed happy was when he was enmeshed in one of those difficult, technical riddles. Then one day it occurred to me why this was so. He had no dreams.

Have dreams, but get up and hustle
when the alarm goes off.

Dream about what you want,
but then *do* something about it.
Never be satisfied with just the dream.

What would you try if you knew for sure
you wouldn't fail?

You have to wake up to make your dreams come true.

Economists

I'VE ALWAYS FELT it takes a special kind of person to be an economist. They are wrong nearly all the time. I mentioned this to a friend of mine who is a very successful economist, pointing out to him that if I was wrong as often as economic predictions are, I would very quickly be out of a job. "Ah, yes," he sighed, "but when you're wrong, people get angry with you. When we're wrong, people are usually relieved."

If all the economists in the world were laid end to end, they would all point in different directions.

Economists use statistics the way drunks use lampposts — more for support than illumination.

If all economists in the world were laid end to end,
they still wouldn't reach a conclusion.

An economist is someone who,
if you lose your telephone number, will estimate for you.

Education

DUE, AS THE SAYING GOES, to circumstances beyond my control, I had to leave school at the age of fourteen after completing grade ten. When I decided to become a chartered accountant, the person who was interviewing me told me I'd never pass the course because I didn't have enough "education." I've often wondered how he felt the day I received a prize for high marks in the final exam (I know he was in the crowd). I do know he was no longer employed by the Institute of Chartered Accountants when I became its president.

What *you* don't know, somebody else
is getting paid for knowing.

The next best thing to knowing a fact
is knowing where to find it.

Education is very much a matter of desire.

Experience, attitude and common sense cannot be taught.

It's not the things you *don't* know that get you in trouble
as much as it is the things you *think* you know but don't.

The person who knows *how* will get a job,
but the person who knows *why* will be the boss.

Reading is to the mind what exercise is to the body.

At least one-quarter of your reading
should be outside your field of work.

To accuse others for your shortcomings shows a lack of
education. To accuse yourself shows that your education
has started. To accuse no one shows it is complete.

There are only two ways to learn:
reading, and being around smarter people.

Don't become educated beyond your intelligence.

Your mind is like your stomach.
It's not what goes into it that counts, but what it digests.

Ignorance is always more expensive than education.

Credentials aren't necessarily accomplishments.

Sometimes it isn't so much what you know
as it is what you can think of quickly.

I'd rather be the *best*-informed than the *most*-informed.

What you don't know may not hurt you,
but it might make you amusing.

If you think school is boring,
wait until you sit around an employment office.

People want to know, but often aren't willing to learn.

Study and get ready. Perhaps your chance will come.

It's what you *do* that counts, not what you know.
People who can solve problems get better jobs
than those who can merely recite facts.
You get paid for using your brains, not for having them.

Intellectuals are people with a lot of knowledge
that no one is willing to pay for.

The lesser the education, the more the suspicion.

Those who *don't* read
have no advantage over those who *can't* read.

Leaders teach others.

When you stop learning, you start to die.

Faith is great, but doubt educates you.

Egotism

DALE CARNEGIE USED TO TELL THE STORY about a man who arrogantly strutted to the podium, clearly intending to show off his superior intelligence and knowledge. After his failed performance, he walked humbly down the aisle and out of the auditorium. Mr. Carnegie observed that had the man approached the podium the way he left it, he could have left it the way he approached it.

Egotism dulls the mind to stupidity.

Under the law of averages,
if you think too much of yourself, others won't.

Ego is the ultimate corrupter.

Feeling you've got it made
is the first step toward getting into a rut.

Never let vanity get in the way of anything
that will do the job better.

The bigger a man's head gets,
the easier it is to fill his shoes.

The egotist says, "Here I am!" Likeable people say,
"There you are!"

Anyone who knows all the answers
isn't being asked the right questions.

The ass who thinks he's a gazelle learns the truth
when he comes to a fence.

Trying to make an impression
is probably the impression you will make.

Today's peacock is tomorrow's feather duster.

Some people grow small trying to be big.

It's better to be missed when you leave
than to be applauded when you arrive.

Don't pay as much attention to what people say
as to what they do.

Sought-after prestige is almost never gotten.
Prestige comes from worthwhile achievements.

Seasickness is a great antidote for a big ego.
A person wanting to vomit doesn't put on airs.

When you think you're all-powerful,
try ordering someone else's dog around.

No matter how big the crowd around you is, remember
that if you were being hanged it would be twice as big.

People who are quick to tell you what they are,
usually aren't.

Don't assume other people have intelligence equal to
yours. They may have more.

If you've earned the right to brag, you don't have to.

Let others find out for themselves how great you are.

Beware the howl of the ego.

Beware of ego demands and emotional extremes.

A lot of problems are caused
by people who need to feel important.

Empathy

THE ELDERS WERE CONSIDERING the misconduct of a deacon. One, urging severe punishment, said, "God has given us eyes." The wiser of the two said, "And he has also given us eyelids."

Punishment should be judged by how far a person has fallen, not by where he landed.

Remember when someone comes to you for help, he likely wouldn't be there if he could handle the problem himself.

You can't walk in another's shoes
without taking off your own.

Problems prepare us to understand the failures of others.

Don't become a party
to someone else trying to prove a point.

It's harder to hide feelings we have
than to fake those we don't.

Enthusiasm

DURING 1972 I TRAVELLED coast to coast in Canada and the United States explaining to audiences, in about thirty or forty cities, the complete reform of the Canadian Income Tax Act.

The first few presentations were fine. I enjoyed giving them, and the audiences received them well. Then I got bored giving the same talk. Soon I noticed the audiences weren't enjoying the talks, either. It was only after I remembered two things about enthusiasm that I, and the audiences, began to enjoy the presentations again. They are: *act* enthusiastic and you'll *be* enthusiastic; and, enthusiasm is as contagious as the measles.

Enthusiasm makes ordinary people extraordinary.

Enthusiastic people enjoy their work more
and get more done.

Enthusiasm turns work into play;
it's hard to imagine succeeding at anything
without having enthusiasm for it.

People with less ability but more enthusiasm will always
outperform people with more ability but less enthusiasm.

Enthusiasm sometimes outperforms intelligence.
The combination is unbeatable.

With whom do you prefer to associate:
an enthusiastic person or one just going through the
motions? Well, others feel the same way about you.

Enthusiasm may have to be faked,
but never for long. Act enthusiastic
and you'll become enthusiastic.

We yearn for many things, but all we really need to be
happy is something to be enthusiastic about.

If you want your organization to flourish,
ensure that the people with power also have enthusiasm.

All successful people have at least
one common characteristic — enthusiasm.

Don't get carried away by temporary enthusiasm.

Look hard enough and you'll find something.

To start from scratch you must have an itch.

To be a truly effective advocate,
you have to have passion for the subject.

By persuading others we sometimes convince ourselves.

You can't convince others
of what you don't believe yourself.

If you're not fired with enthusiasm,
maybe you'll just be fired.

Evils

As with the temperature, there are degrees of evil. And just as the sun and the wind can affect the temperature on any given day, there are forces, such as alcohol, drugs, greed and selfishness, that affect the level of evil in given circumstances. To conquer evil we must defeat the forces.

A major disadvantage of drinking too much
is that you mistake words for thoughts.

When choosing between two evils,
pick the one you haven't tried before.

We destroy good by sparing evil.

The surest way to encourage evil is to give in to it.

Alcohol doesn't help you do anything better;
it just makes you less ashamed of doing things badly.

When faced with evil,
people of character do not remain neutral.

The only thing necessary for the triumph of evil
is for good people to do nothing.

No one ever became evil all at once.

Excuses

REASONS ARE OFTEN JUST EXCUSES, and I've always had difficulty excusing excuses. Like most of you, I've heard some very good ones and some very bad ones in my day. Probably the worst I ever heard was one evening when my father didn't want my older brother to have our old wreck of a car. The "reason" he gave was that the horn wasn't working. The main problem with this "excuse" was that my brother merely wanted to practise driving in a vacant field out behind our house.

Don't make excuses — make good.

People who are good at making excuses
are rarely any good at anything else.

An achiever will find a way. Others will find an excuse.

No excuse is good enough to be called a reason.

Loafing is its own excuse.

Those who want badly to do something, find ways;
those who want badly not to do something, find excuses.

You can't improve by making excuses.

You become a failure
when you start to blame others.

Inferior people make excuses for their faults;
superior people correct them.

Executives

I'M NOT SURE OF THE EXACT DATE this took place, but it was clearly the day that I realized that being an executive depended more on what you have to do than on what your title is. We had a very serious employee problem. Money had been stolen. I was the one the problem was given to. It dawned on me that I had become an executive when I realized that I, and no one else, was going to have to decide what to do.

The higher you climb up the executive ladder,
the more you will be judged by how well you lead others.

Managers think about this week.
Executives think about next year.

Those who enjoy responsibility tend to get it.
Those who simply like authority usually lose it.

Doing a job well yourself is one thing; getting others to do
a job well is something else.

To gain respect as an executive, become known
as someone who doesn't get in other people's way.

Executives distinguish between problems
and things that simply annoy them.

Anything that increases employees' pride and satisfaction
in their work will increase their enthusiasm
for making things even better.
Good executives never let improvements go unnoticed.

A good executive makes problems so interesting
that everyone wants to work on them.

Executives set themselves above their employees
only in assuming responsibility.

As an executive, what happens when you're not there
may well be more important than what happens
when you are there.

Don't confuse authority with power.

Delegate, but don't abdicate.

Good executives find out *what* went wrong, not *who*.

Executives who have competent people don't bother
them with too much supervision.
Distinguish between leadership and interference.

Ask for *specific* results and you'll get *better* results.

There's rarely growth without delegation.
Without delegation there cannot be effective management.

When one of your people makes their first mistake in a
long while — congratulate them on the long while.

Good tries have to be praised as much as wins.

It takes a different type of person to run a business than it
does to start one. Entrepreneurs aren't good executives,
and vice versa.

When someone is doing his best,
give him lots of chances. How many chances
would you give a baby to walk before giving up?

The tougher the problems,
the higher paid are the executives who solve them.

No amount of success at work
can compensate for failure at home.

There's always room at the top.
Many who get there fall asleep and roll off.

No matter how far up the executive ladder you go,
somewhere you have a boss.

Management is climbing a ladder. Leadership is knowing
the ladder is leaning against the right wall.

The only job where you start at the top is digging a hole.

The best executives build such effective organizations
that they can function well without them.

Experience

EARLIER IN THE BOOK, under the heading "Boredom and Bores," I talked about the job I once had sorting sheets of paper (waybills at a railway company, actually) into numerical order.

After about three weeks at this job I approached my supervisor and asked for something more challenging. He suggested I stay at the sorting job for another couple of weeks, saying that the extra "experience" would do me good. It was then that I realized I would not have five *weeks'* experience at the end of this time, but rather one *day's* experience twenty-five times over.

Life is one continuous learning experience.

Nothing upsets a theory like experience.

Experience often teaches us things we don't want to know.

Experience doesn't always produce expertise.
Sometimes it merely produces bias.

Experience is a guide post, not a hitching post.

One thing tougher than learning from experience
is not learning from experience.

You don't let a fox guard the chickens
just because he has experience in the hen house.

Experience is what you think you have until you get more.

Experience includes knowing the things you shouldn't do.

You can't learn how to swim by reading a book.
You have to jump into the water and get wet.

The problem with experience is that
you rarely have it at the time you need it most.

Experience is a tough school.
You get the test first and the lesson later.

If you've had a bull by the horns,
you know a few more things than anyone who hasn't.

The secret of walking on water
is knowing where the stones are.

Stick around long enough and you'll see everything —
at least twice.

You'll find your wisdom teeth
the first time you bite off more than you can chew.

Experience is not what happens to you;
it is what you *do* with what happens to you.

Considering the cost of experience,
it *should* be the best teacher.

Experience is another name for mistakes.

Proverbs are short sentences based on long experience.

Experience often results from expecting something else.

You may get a big surprise by reading the small print,
but you might get a bigger one if you don't.

Experience tells you that you've made that mistake before.

If an old pro takes enough interest in you to
pass along a few tips — listen.

The problem with never having played the game
is that you don't know what goes on in players' minds.

Wisdom includes learning from every experience.

People become wise by learning from what happens to
them when they aren't.

Wisdom comes from good judgement which comes from
experience which often comes from bad judgement.

Trivial things can be very emotional because of particular
past experiences.

The worst example can be the best teacher.
Do the opposite.

Don't let experiences limit your vision.

Relying only on our own experience
may mean we don't have enough information.

Failure

I REMEMBER ALMOST NONE of the British history which was a mandatory subject when I attended grade school — perhaps it still is, but I doubt it. However, one story still remains vivid in my mind. It is about Robert the Bruce lying in his bunk, having decided he had failed miserably after many attempts to defeat his hated enemy. He was watching a spider trying to attach a web across a difficult corner. The spider tried six times without success, then on the seventh try the web was successfully attached, inspiring Robert to try one more time. He did. He won.

Few plan to fail, but many fail to plan.

If you're made of the right stuff,
a hard fall results in a high bounce.

The only time you can really fail is the last time you try.

When you do something on a regular basis,
the chances for an occasional failure are enormous.

People can't walk over you until you lie down.

Failure is never fatal and success is never final.

If an experiment fails, find out *why*.
It may have nothing to do with the merits of the cause.

Failure is not falling down — it's staying down.

Occasional failure is the price of improvement.

Two classes of failures: People who thought and never did,
and people who did and never thought.

Never be afraid of falling on your face;
it proves you were moving forward.

Short-term failures should never spoil long-term goals.

A set-back while doing something right is still a win.

Failure isn't failure if you learn from it.

If you always try, you will sometimes fail.

You might be disappointed if you fail,
but you're doomed if you don't at least try.

Faults

DALE CARNEGIE HAD A WONDERFUL ATTITUDE when it came to reacting to anyone who faulted him. He would say, "If my critic had known about all my other faults, he would have criticized me much more severely than he did."

We find faults in others that we don't see in ourselves.

Admitting a fault
doesn't mean you don't have to correct it.

Many of our faults are more forgivable
than the ways in which we try to hide them.

We can't correct all our faults at once.
Work on one at a time.

The greatest fault is to think you have none.

The way some people find fault,
you'd think there was a reward.

If you admit you have faults,
you will deprive others of the pleasure
of pointing them out.

Those who admit their faults have one less fault to admit.

Fear

BECAUSE OF MY LACK OF FORMAL EDUCATION, I was a provisional student in the course leading to the designation of *chartered accountant*. The provision was that if I failed an exam, I was out. Walking into the room to write my first exam, I was almost paralyzed by fear. Then I remembered Roosevelt's admonition that the only thing we had to fear was fear itself. Did I know enough to pass the exam? Probably. Was there anyone there who was trying to prevent me from passing? Definitely not. Was I writing the same examination as everyone else in the room? Yes. So, what was there to be afraid of other than fear itself? Nothing.

A good scare is often more effective than good advice.

Fear is a protection — panic isn't.

There is nothing to be feared like scared people.

Fear defeats more people than anything else in the world.

Frightened people talk too much.

If you know you can do it, there's no need to be afraid.

Common sense gets a lot of credit
that really belongs to cold feet.

Don't be afraid to make a big move if one is needed.
Chasms can't be crossed in two small jumps.

Fear is a darkroom in which negatives are developed.

There are far more fears than dangers.

Sometimes it's better to panic beforehand and be calm
when "it" happens, than to be calm beforehand
and panic when "it" happens.

Only the way you think determines courage or fear.
The best way to beat fear is to do the thing you fear
over and over again.

Fear exists only in the mind.

Keep your fears to yourself —
share your courage with others.

Trust your hopes, not your fears.

Fools

P.T. BARNUM SAID there was one born every minute. My mother always said there were no fools — just people who did foolish things. I think they were both right. There's at least one person born every minute, and every last one of us does foolish things from time to time. To be certifiable as a fool, I think I would have to do foolish things all the time.

He that is taught only by himself has a fool for a teacher.

A wise man changes his mind; a fool never.

Even if thousands of people say something foolish,
it is still something foolish.

Even fools are occasionally right.

Only a fool would resolve not to go into the water
until he had learned to swim.

If you're arguing with a fool,
be sure he isn't doing the same thing.

There's a bigger fool than the person who thinks he knows
everything; it's the person who argues with him.

The wise learn from mistakes; fools repeat them.

Friendship

I LIVE IN TORONTO. Lou lives in Ottawa. We both have professional and family responsibilities. Neither of us would normally have any reason to go to Winnipeg. But I know if I called him tonight and said nothing more than that it was imperative that we meet in Winnipeg next Tuesday, he would be there, no questions asked. How do I know? Simple. Because if he made the call, I'd be there.

Short memories make long friendships.

To destroy an enemy, make him your friend.

When a friend achieves something,
praise him; both your lives will be richer for it.

Friends stick with you when you're wrong.
Anybody will back you when you're right.

Allow friends their peculiarities.

Friendship includes loving people more than they deserve.

When silence between two people is comfortable,
they're true friends.

When you make a fool of yourself,
real friends know it isn't permanent.

A mutual enemy is a strong bond of friendship.

People who don't want to really *know* you,
but just want to know *about* you, aren't friends.

Real friends know all about you and still like you.

Don't make everything a test of friendship.

Real friends don't prop up your weaknesses —
they encourage your strengths.

The blows of a friend
should be preferable to the kisses of an enemy.

You don't really make friends, you recognize them.

The difference between friends and acquaintances
is that friends help whereas acquaintances give advice.

To make friends,
become sincerely interested in other people.

If we knew all about them, we would see enough sorrow
and suffering in most people's lives to make us like them.

Making friends is easy. It's keeping them that's tough.

Real friends multiply joys and divide grief.

A real friend comes in when others are going out.

The only way to have a friend is to be one.

Having friends
depends almost entirely on your own behaviour.

Sympathy says, "I'm sorry."
Friendship asks, "How can I help?"

Minor disagreements should never be allowed
to spoil major friendships.

Short visits enhance long friendships.

Friendship is a savings account.
If you don't make deposits,
there will be nothing to withdraw.

To have lasting friendships,
what's important to your friends
has to be as important to you as their friendship is.

A friend's honest point of view
should add strength to the friendship.

Believe someone is a good friend,
and you'll treat him one way.
But, believe he has become your enemy
and your treatment will change.
Yet there may have been no change at all in him,
but only a change in your attitude.

If you think you can get along without others,
you are wrong. But if you think that others can't get along
without you, you're even more wrong.

Friends are always more important than things.

Never pass up a chance
to defend someone who's not present.

Demand that your friends be perfect
on the day *you* become perfect.

The person who always agrees with you
will probably be the first to really stick it to you.

Treat your friends like family and your family like friends.

We need to realize that even our friends
will sometimes let us down.

It's easy to tell who your best friend is:
It's the person who brings out the best in you.

Goals

WHEN I STARTED TO WORK full-time back in 1953, there was no such thing as job security. Feeling that I could always find another job in a week, I set a goal of saving enough money to cover my expenses for seven days. When I reached that, I then set one of being able to live for two weeks, then three weeks, a month, and so on. I was, at a very young age, actually setting retirement goals. But had I started out with the goal of saving enough money on which to retire, I would have become discouraged and abandoned the process very early on. But by setting a realistic goal, and then setting another realistic goal once the previous one was reached, I learned the right way to approach the goal-setting process.

Our goals must be within the bounds of ability.
Otherwise, we'll constantly be frustrated.

Goals should be difficult but not impossible.
Otherwise, we'll give up after a few tries.

Don't worry about achieving perfection,
but always strive for it.

It's better to aim for perfection
and miss than to hit imperfection.

Don't worry about topping others,
but always try to top yourself.

Set a realistic goal and, when it's reached,
set another a little bit higher.

When what we did yesterday becomes more important
than what we plan to do tomorrow,
it's time to set a new goal.

Poorly defined goals lead to carelessness and boredom.

Napoleon said, "If you set out to take Vienna —
take Vienna."

When you feel defeated,
set some easy goals and work your way back up.

Don't let short-term failures hamper long-term goals.

Long-range goals offset short-term setbacks.

An obstacle is what you see
when you take your eye off your goal.

People with specific goals work harder to achieve them.

A good goal to set is to define what you're going to do
when you can't do what you're doing now.

People with goals are always potentially successful. There
are so few of them that there's hardly any competition.

Recognize the difference between wants and needs
and then reconcile them.

If you don't have a plan of your own,
you're apt to be a part of someone else's.

Long-term goals have to be broken down into short-term
sub-goals; and there have to be rewards along the way.

There are no shortcuts to any place worth getting to.

Goals without timetables aren't really goals.

If you don't know where you're going,
how will you know when you get there?

There's little point in aiming for something
unless you intend to pull the trigger.

People who don't know where they're going
usually end up somewhere else.

When working to reach a goal you really want, you can't
be doing a lot of incompatible things at the same time.

We can only act one day at a time,
but we can think mid-term and plan long-term.

Limit your subjects.

In goal setting, it's not as important to know where things
are now as to know where they're going to be.

Don't try to make circumstances fit your goals.
Make your goals fit the circumstances.

After you throw your hat over the wall, climb it.

When you see the light, don't turn down the wick.

Gossip

IF YOU WANT to get someone's undivided attention, don't yell at them. Rather, sidle up to them and quietly say, "Psst, listen to this." They'll be all ears.

Great minds discuss ideas.
Average minds discuss events. Little minds gossip.

Where there is whispering, there is lying.

There is no such thing as an idle rumour.

Middle management is where you still hear the gossip, but you're not high enough to know whether it's true.

Who gossips *to* you will gossip *about* you.

Conversation exercises the mind.
Gossip only exercises the tongue.

Always discourage gossip.

Nothing makes a long story short
like the arrival of the person you're talking about.

The only right thing to do behind someone's back
is to pat it.

Government

MY FORMER COLLEAGUE, the late Frank Sanders, swears this is true. In his native Austria, World War Two pensioners had to report to a government office in person on the last day of each month to pick up their pension cheques. Apparently this procedure was instituted after the government discovered that cheques made out to people who had died continued to be cashed. Frank's friend, Hans, missed his February 28th pick-up because he had the flu. When he went in on March 31st to get both cheques, the clerk would only give him the March cheque because "he had no proof that Hans had been alive on February 28th."

In government there's always one more jackass
than you bargained for.

Inflation is how governments tax poor people.

Governments can't create something out of nothing.
Anything a government does
is paid for by taxpayer's money.

A state can't survive if everyone is free to obey the law
or not according to his personal opinion.

Even crime wouldn't pay if the government ran it.

All government programs have three things in common:
a start, a middle and no end.

It's impossible to support governments
in the style to which they've become accustomed.

The natural cynicism of the marketplace
is preferable to the naive optimism of governments.

Nothing heals faster than a tax cut.

Habits

IT'S FUNNY HOW HABITS GET FORMED and what's sometimes read into them. Athletes are notorious for having habits based on superstition. When I started to play Junior B hockey in Toronto, the coach noticed that I always put a towel inside the knee of my right goalie pad.

After getting new pads, I stopped using the towel, and when the team hit a bit of a slump, the main cause of which the coach figured was me, he told me to put the towel back in my pad again. I've never had the heart to tell him the only reason I started doing it in the first place was because our cat had urinated on the inside of the old pad.

Act the way you'd like to be and after a while
you'll be the way you act.

Habits are more reliable than memory.

Repeating the act reinforces the habit.

Form the habit of doing the right things
and you will do well even when not at your best.

At age twenty, genes provide your face.
At age forty, though, *you've* decided what you look like.

A good habit is to do at least one thing every day
that you don't want to do.

Keep doing what you're doing
and you're going to keep getting what you're getting.

You can't carry on all your old habits
and expect different results.

The best way to break a bad habit is to drop it.

When the only tool you have is a hammer,
you tend to treat everything like a nail.

To break a habit you have to convince yourself
that what you want later is more important
than what you want now.

What we do when we don't have to will determine
what we'll do when we can't help ourselves.

If you've been doing something the same way
for a long time, the odds are there's a better way to do it.

Happiness

DURING A LULL in the poker game I was expounding on the fact that my wife and children were the centre of my happiness. I turned to Al, a perfectly happy life-long bachelor, and asked him why he never got married. "Well," he said with uncommon candour, "anybody I ever wanted didn't want me. And I always figured I was better off wanting something I didn't have than having something I didn't want."

Happiness is good health and a bad memory.

Most people pursue happiness — the wise create it.

The time to be happy is now;
the place to be happy is here.

A sure route to happiness is to make others happy.

We don't laugh because we are happy;
we are happy because we laugh.

Happiness is a by-product.

Live so that your happiness depends as little as possible on
external things.

Happiness begins with a leisurely breakfast.

Happiness is not a place at which to arrive; it's a means of
travelling.

Happiness can't be saved up. It has to be used every day.

Happiness is a lot like a butterfly. The more we chase it,
the more it eludes us. But forget about it and it might
alight on our shoulders.

To do without some of the things we want
is a necessary component of happiness.

If we never knew sadness,
we couldn't recognize happiness.

True happiness can come only from yourself.

Success is getting what you want.
Happiness is wanting what you get.

Happiness makes up in depth what it lacks in length.

If you want happiness, don't expect the absence of conflict;
develop the ability to cope with it.

Avoid people who make you unhappy.

Happiness is your own responsibility.

A busy person doesn't have time to be unhappy.

There can be no true happiness without a clear conscience.

Happiness is a choice, not a response.

If you have someone to love, something to do,
and something to hope for, you should be happy.

Once you identify what bothers you,
you have two choices: do something about it or learn to
live with it; either beats living in constant unhappiness.

We always add to or subtract from the happiness
of everyone with whom we come in contact,
and which we do is almost always within our control.

No matter how tough times look,
they'll look better with a cheerful approach.

Have you ever seen a perfectly happy perfectionist?

Happiness is often a sign of wisdom.

A happy person isn't a person in the right circumstances;
it's a person with the right attitude.

Happiness comes from appreciating what we have,
instead of being miserable about what we don't have.

You've found true happiness when ordinary things are
made into extraordinary pleasures.

Happy people don't *have* the best of everything;
they just *make* the best of everything.

Find happiness in your work
or you may never find it anywhere.

Look for your joys in simple things.

Heroes and Heroism

IT'S USUALLY WISE to have a number of heroes in your life because some of them are bound to let you down; and when they do, it's wiser still to remember that they didn't volunteer for the job in the first place. Heroes are usually the product of being in a particular place, at a particular time, in a particular set of circumstances. Absolutely no one can be a hero all the time; the responsibility is simply too awesome.

We can't all be heroes.
Someone has to stand on the sidelines and cheer.

Concentrate on what you're doing
and the applause will come.

Most of us will never do great things,
but we can do small things in a great way.

Responsibility is one price of greatness.

Triumph is just *umph* added to *try*.

Don't look for praise.
Do your best and be patient — praise will come.

Try too hard to be a hero and you may end up a zero.

Heroism can't be planned.

Honesty

WHEN I WAS AN ACCOUNTING STUDENT, one of the jobs I had to do for a while was to periodically count the cash at an auto parts store and reconcile it to the amount of sales reported. The problem was the owner would often take cash out of the register and not tell anyone. One day my boss gave him a convincing lecture on the importance of leaving a note indicating the amount he had taken. The next time I went in to count the cash, there was the note. It said, "Dear Lyman, I took it all."

Being insincere uses up a lot of energy.
That's why so much social life is exhausting.

Be an honest person and you will know there's one less deceiver in the world.

A person who will steal *for* me will steal *from* me.

You can't change your ethics according to circumstances.

Always bet on integrity over cleverness.

There are *no* degrees of honesty,
but limitless degrees of dishonesty.

Better to be the guy who bought the
Brooklyn Bridge than the one who sold it.

If you can't say no, yes doesn't mean anything.

To be trusted, be trustworthy.

Pure motives are better than good moves.

When in doubt, tell the truth.

Better to be disliked for what you believe in
than to be liked for what you don't.

The right thing to do is always simple and direct.

You can occasionally fool others,
but you can never fool yourself.

Excessive flattery will eventually be taken
for exactly what it is: a phoney gesture.

You can't fool all the people all the time
because some of them are busy fooling you.

Don't tell me what I *want* to hear.
Tell me what I *ought* to hear.

We tend to believe strangers
because they've never deceived us.

Better to fail with honour than succeed by fraud.

Sometimes it isn't *doing* what's right that's the problem,
it's *knowing* what's right.

When trying to persuade people,
tell them only what they'll believe.

For every credibility gap there is a gullibility fill.

Honest people never try to be something they aren't.

Hope

I'VE KNOWN PERSONALLY two people who spent most of the war in prisoner-of-war camps — one in Asia and the other in Germany. They didn't know each other, but they clearly shared a common characteristic — they knew the importance of hope. Both of them told me that hope was the only thing that kept them, and thousands like them, going.

Hope is the little feeling you have
that the big feeling you're having is temporary.

There's always time to start over again.

Leadership often consists solely of keeping hope alive.

You can't turn back the clock.
But you can wind it up again.

You can't erase the past, but you can record over it.

Learn from yesterday; live today; hope for tomorrow.

You can't go back and make a new start.
But you can start now to make a new ending.

Human Nature

IT'S AN INTERESTING TERM — "human nature." It encompasses almost as many natures as there are humans. A lot of human nature is good, some of it is bad. It's been said that human nature is what sets us apart from animals. Do we learn it, or are we born with it? Can it change within a single human being? It's a great mystery and a wonderful excuse.

Human nature is what makes you swear at a pedestrian when driving, and swear at the driver when walking.

You're unique — so is everyone else.

The difference between conviction and prejudice is that a conviction can be explained without a loss of temper.

It's easy to see both sides
of issues we don't really care about it.

In a battle between logic and emotion,
emotion will win almost every time.

People respond well to anything that confirms
their self-images. They also respond poorly to anything
that conflicts with their self-images.

When a person lowers his voice,
he wants something; when he raises it, he didn't get it.

What we see may depend on what we look for.

Every want isn't a need.

Many people don't know exactly what they want,
but they're sure they don't have it.

What's important to people
is whatever they think is important.

The deepest human craving is for appreciation.

Each generation has to find out for itself
that the stove is hot.

Everyone is self-made, but only successful people admit it.

When someone slaps you on the back,
he may be trying to get you to swallow something.

Flattery should be like chewing gum.
Enjoy it for a while, but don't swallow it.

Being yourself is easy. Being what other people
want you to be is so hard you shouldn't even try.

Beware of the person who has nothing to lose.

A good way to judge people
is to watch what they do with what they have.

Too many coincidences aren't a coincidence.

The village idiot sometimes asks the toughest questions.

If people aren't dealt with as individuals,
they eventually rebel.

Humour

UNTIL ABOUT 1985, I think I could honestly say that every single person with whom I'd spent more than a few hours, at one time or another showed a sense of humour. But since then I've known a number of completely humourless people. What in Heaven's name has caused this great loss? Probably *political correctness*, that great cure for which there's no known disease.

Having no sense of humour is like being a car with no shocks; every little pothole jolts you.

It's good to be the first to laugh at yourself.

Life can still be funny when people die, just as it stays being serious when people laugh.

If you don't have a sense of humour,
you may have no sense at all.

Ideas

WE ALL COME UP with lots of great ideas throughout our lives. The problem is that we seldom come up with them at the right time or in the right place, so they are forgotten. The great idea that came to us in the shower gets washed down the drain by the next thought that squeezes it out. Now, here's an idea: Keep an "Idea Book." Put in it every idea that comes to you. Treat it like a diary. You'll be amazed how many good ideas will eventually find their way in there.

Ideas are useless until acted upon.

An idea is like a train: if you don't board it while it's there, you'll miss it.

Ideas shouldn't be blamed for their own corruption.

The best way to come up with a great idea
is to hatch a lot of ideas and eliminate the bad ones.

You can't master an idea until you can express it clearly.

Even the best ideas have to be packaged and sold.

Great ideas need landing gear as well as wings.

Ideas, like wheelbarrows, don't go anywhere on their own.

New ideas are more acceptable
when presented in bite-size pieces.

Ideas are like children. Yours are special.

Intelligence

UNCLE ART NEVER ATTENDED SCHOOL. Not even for one day. Yet he taught himself to read and write and made a living weighing fish. The scale he used was an old-fashioned kind where the weight was determined by sliding a marker along a bar. Many times I watched in awe as he hefted a crate of fish onto the scale and, with his first attempt, set the marker in exactly the right notch, meaning he had known the weight almost to the ounce.

Stopping to think is a good sign of intelligence.

Intelligence allows us to cope with stupidity.

Intelligence enables some people
to get by without education.

Rather than know all the answers,
ask really good questions.

The more intelligence you use, the less material you need.

One computer can replace hundreds of ordinary people;
a thousand computers
can't replace one extraordinarily intelligent person.

Intelligence can be more important than knowledge.

Intelligent people aim at things no one else sees —
and hits them.

It takes more intelligence to find out what *isn't* wrong
than to find out what *is* wrong.

We're all ignorant, but on different subjects.

We rarely forget what we figure out ourselves.

Many are surprised
at how much uneducated people know.

When you don't know much,
you've got to use your brains.

Judgement

I SPENT THE SUMMER OF 1958 in Saskatchewan. One of the people I befriended out there lived on a ranch. We accompanied his father to a livestock sale and I watched him, seemingly just by looking them over, buy about a dozen animals. At the end of the auction the animals were grouped according to buyer. It was clear my friend's father had selected the best of the lot, although that wasn't obvious as he picked them from the original, large herd. When I asked him how he made his selections he said, "I just use my judgement." I asked him if he could explain that in a little more detail. "No," he replied.

We judge ourselves by what we think we can do,
but others judge us by what we can actually do.

If you put your best foot forward,
at least it won't be in your mouth.

Sometimes it's better to let nature take its course
than to adhere to hard, fast rules.

Know when to take a risk without risking all.

Kindness

My father had died and I didn't have enough money for a plane ticket home, and taking the train or the bus would take too long. I knocked on the office door of the very important businessman and asked him if he would lend me the equivalent of what was then a month's pay. I had no collateral. I didn't know how long it would take me to pay it back. Without a signed note or I.O.U. he gave me the money. I wish I could tell you his name — you'd probably recognize it — but the only condition of the interest-free loan was that I never tell anyone about it. I don't think this breaks the promise.

Encouragement after a failure
is worth more than a medal after success.

Be better to your neighbours,
and you'll have better neighbours.

You can repay debts of goods or money,
but you forever owe people who are kind to you.

A small kindness to one person is more useful
than a great love for humanity.

When you have a kind thought, express it.
You'll never be sorry you did.

Sow kindness, reap friendship.

One loving act is worth a thousand wonderful sentiments.

When you think of a nice thing to do for someone, do it!

To make life worthwhile, make one person happy today.

Treat everyone you meet
as though it were *their* last day on earth.

Be kind. Everyone you meet is fighting a tough battle.

An ounce of kindness is worth a ton of cleverness.

Whatever the circumstances,
finding a way to say thanks always enhances life.

If you were arrested for kindness,
would there be enough evidence to convict you?

Never pass up a chance to say a kind word.

Leadership

LEADERSHIP IMPLIES A TEAM SITUATION. It involves performance. I've seen more examples of true leadership in hockey games than in any other scenario. Probably the greatest sixty minutes of leadership in that sport took place on March 23, 1944. (Yes, I'm old enough to remember it.) Maurice "Rocket" Richard, of the Montreal Canadiens, scored all five goals in a 5-1 win over arch rivals, the Toronto Maple Leafs. What made this feat of leadership even more impressive was the fact it took place during the Stanley Cup semi-finals.

Leaders build reputations by developing other people's skills and talents.

Leaders get average people to do superior work.

The effective delegation of authority
is a mark of leadership.

One test of leadership is to see if anyone is following.
Without followers, there are no leaders.

People who can't lead and won't follow
make great speed bumps.

Leadership includes getting people to work
when they don't have to.

Good leaders inspire confidence in themselves.
Great leaders inspire confidence in others.

Leaders don't waste time trying to lay blame.

Pull a rope and it will follow you. Push it and it will curl
up and go nowhere. It's the same with leading people.

The best way to give people responsibility
is to let them know you trust them.

A leader's job is to help others
make the most of themselves.

Leadership includes changing people from what they are
to what they should be.

Leaders have two important characteristics:
they're going somewhere
and they're able to persuade others to go with them.

Leaders are approachable and easy to talk to.

Leaders always show consideration
for the feelings of others.

Asking who should be the leader
is like asking who ought to sing tenor in the quartet.
It should be the person who *can* sing tenor.

A leader is a person
who has earned the right to have a follower.

Leadership is getting others to do things because
they want to do them.

Leadership is action, not position.

You don't have to be brilliant to be a good leader,
but you do have to understand how people feel
and what motivates them.

Leaders must first know how to handle themselves.

Leaders can't worry about the possible negative results of
all their actions. If they do, they should be taking orders,
not giving them.

If you can't lead, follow! If you won't follow,
at least get out of the way.

Leaders stay in character, being themselves at all times.

Leaders act like coaches, not like quarterbacks.

Leaders help people to do a better job,
but they will never do it for them.

When the great leader's work is done, everyone says,
"*We* did it!"

Leaders rely on reason and persuasion,
not on ordering people around.

Leaders avoid trying to act
like they think leaders should act.

Leaders issue one warning, then they act.

Followers seek methods and precedents.
Leaders seek solutions.

Leaders make difficult things seem simple,
not simple things seem difficult.

Action makes leaders, not knowledge.

Leaders make everyone else feel important.

You can't be followed by the crowd if *you're* following *it*.

Leaders take more than their share of blame
and less than their share of credit.

Truly effective leadership produces leaders
as well as followers.

The leader's role is not to change people.
It's to put people's strengths to work.

Leadership is a dialogue, not a monologue.

Leaders know the way, go the way, and show the way.

Ordinary people focus on doing things right,
leaders on doing the right thing.

True leadership must benefit the followers.

Independent people who can't think interdependently
don't make leaders.

Leaders respect the rights and worth of everyone, always
treating people as equals, never as inferior.

Leaders tell people how they're doing before being asked.

Leaders look upon themselves as members of the team.

Leaders instil purpose.

Leaders give everyone a vital role.

Leaders understand that the occasional disappointment
is the price of progress, so they keep trying.

Leadership means doing what is necessary,
not just what is popular.

Leaders don't fly off the handle.

Leaders listen.

Leaders keep their preconceptions
and personal likes and dislikes out of their decisions.

Leaders have goals; followers have wishes.

Lies

THERE ARE MANY REASONS why lying should be avoided, including the morality of the situation, but I learned a very practical reason to avoid lying when I was in grade school. I was present when one of my classmates gave his excuses to the teacher for not having his homework done — for the third time that week. I was also present the following Saturday when our teacher came to his house to talk to his parents. I was asked to wait outside. He emerged a few minutes later, obviously having been punished. But his logic has stayed with me ever since. "You know," he said, "I just don't have a good enough memory to be a liar."

Lies may cover the present, but they have no future.

Lies travel faster than truth, but they don't stay as long.

A lie travels around the county
while the truth is tying its shoelaces.

Always read between the lies.

A good lie finds more believers than a bad truth.

Life

OF THE THOUSANDS OF COMMERCIALS I heard on the radio as a kid (I was, and am, an inveterate radio listener), there is one that stands out loud and clear in my memory. It was for a product called "Carter's little liver pills." I'm pretty sure the adjective "little" was intended to modify pills rather than livers. Anyway, the reason I remember it so well is the line "If life's not worth living, it may be the liver."

Life is like a trombone.
Put nothing in it and you get nothing out of it.

Life is like a taxi ride.
Whether you're going anywhere or not,
the meter keeps ticking.

There's always going to be good news.

We can't choose how or when we're going to die.
We *can* choose how we're going to live.

There's not much you can do about the length of your life,
but you can do a lot about its depth.

You can be accidentally born a lady or a gentleman,
but you have to work at dying one.

Life is like riding a bicycle;
you don't fall off unless you stop pedalling.

Desire is the key in any endeavour.

Every right carries with it a responsibility;
every opportunity an obligation; every possession a duty.

Don't be a person without a signature.

It'll be interesting to see how long the meek keep the earth
after they inherit it.

There isn't enough darkness in the world
to extinguish the light from one small candle.

Everything that lives has the power to become greater.

We didn't inherit the earth from our ancestors;
we borrowed it from our children.

Don't be the first to break family tradition.

Opportunity isn't in your environment — it's in *you*.

The difference between a groove
and a rut is sometimes pretty slight.

Freedom has two sides: privilege on one
and responsibility on the other. Privilege isn't on both.

The future is going to happen,
so we may as well try to influence it positively.

Don't count your days, make your days count.

It's not the difficulties we have to face,
but the attitude with which we face them
that determines the quality of our lives.

Little streams make oceans. Tiny grains of sand make beaches.
We're all important in the large scheme of things.

Never before in the history of the earth
has there been anyone exactly like you;
there is no one exactly like you right now;
there never will be anyone exactly like you again.

Neither success nor failure is usually final.

When you get what you want,
remember how much you wanted it.

To live with a weakness, neither hate it nor justify it.

People aren't so much against *you*
as they are *for* themselves.

Hunger is the best sauce.

Helping others is all life is really about.

Life clearly includes "if."

The world owes no one a living,
but it owes us all an *opportunity* to make a living.

What hasn't happened in the last twenty *years*
can happen in the next twenty *seconds*.

Inch by inch, life's a cinch. Yard by yard, it's very hard.

If you walk down a pier, you're apt to see dead fish.

There's a big difference
between real suffering and false martyrdom.

Common sense is so rare
that it's often mistaken for genius.

Freedom is the right to *be* wrong,
not the right to *do* wrong.

Listening

BACK IN THE FIFTIES, I developed the bad habit of continuing to work at whatever I was doing while others talked to me. I did hear everything they said, and thought I was being very efficient. This ended one day when a young lady was telling me about a problem she was having that she thought I might be able to help her with. I continued drafting a letter while she talked. Suddenly she shouted "You're not listening!" I assured her I was, and thought I proved it by repeating almost everything she had said. "But," she said, "your eyes weren't."

Most people wouldn't listen at all if they didn't think it was their turn next.

When you hear generalities, ask specific questions.
That way you'll find out what's really being said.

It's more important to be able to listen well in one language
than it is to be able to speak ten.

Listening is all you need to do to entertain most people.

When we're talking we can only repeat what we know.
By listening we learn what others know.

Good listeners aren't just popular; they get to know things.

Thoughts are worth more than money.
If we exchange a dollar, we still only have a dollar each.
But when we exchange ideas, each of us has one more idea.

Nothing makes people better listeners
than hearing their names.

It sometimes takes courage to speak up.
Sometimes it also takes courage to just listen.

Applause is the only interruption that's ever appreciated.

Listen to everyone. Everyone has ideas.

Good listening needs your undivided attention.

Don't listen to decide what *you're* going to say.
Listen to understand what the other person is saying.

Don't fall into the trap of hearing only the first few words
of a sentence because you're finishing it in your own mind.

Don't tune out people
simply because you don't like something about them.

Don't overreact to ideas that question your beliefs.

Listen for *in*tent as well as *con*tent.

Listen to what people *say*, but don't neglect clues indicating
how they *feel* — such as body language,
facial expression and tone of voice.

The other side of listening-too-little is talking too much.

While listening,
withhold judgement until you hear everything.

If we listened better, history wouldn't have to repeat itself.

Leaders listen.

Lost Causes

SHE WAS THE RUNT OF THE LITTER. She had hip problems, eye problems, ear problems, heart problems; and she couldn't eat on her own. She couldn't even bark. She was in such bad shape that the breeder let us have her for the vet fee. Our older son, Matthew, fed her by hand, three times a day, for almost a year before she learned to eat by herself. We *all* fed her a load of love. And although she never grew to more than about one-quarter the size of a normal Cavalier King Charles Spaniel, right now, over ten years later, as I'm writing this, Roxy is barking for her supper.

If your boat is doomed to sink, look forward to the swim.

Make everything a life-and-death proposition
and you're going to be dead a lot.

Accept what's achievable rather than crave the impossible.

Even if we aren't going to be around to pick the fruit,
we still have to plant some trees.

Nothing will ever be tried
if all objections must first be overcome.

If you lay an egg, stand back and admire it.

If you have a lemon, make lemonade.

There's no point putting silk stockings on a pig.

Trying to teach a pig to sing is a waste of time,
and it annoys the pig.

The trouble with wrestling with a pig
is not just that you get dirty, but the pig likes it.

Few situations are really hopeless.

If you feel you can't go on any longer, go downtown,
find someone who needs help and help that person.

If you get away to a bad start, be sure you don't taper off.

We can't control what happens to us,
but we can control how we face up to it.

The first law of holes: If you're in one, stop digging.

Before giving up,
imagine the objective being achieved by someone you hate.

There are two kinds of people who seldom amount to much:
those who won't do what they're told,
and those who do only what they're told.

Luck

I WAS BACK HOME in Prince Edward Island for a holiday when I met an old-timer I hadn't seen since I first left P.E.I. about fourteen years earlier. I'd always had a job during that time and had continually taken courses, including the gruelling four years leading up to my C.A. designation. The old-timer asked me what I was doing in Toronto. I told him I was working for an accounting firm. "Humpf," he snorted, or something that sounded like that, "you're sure *lucky* to have steady work."

Few things are as dangerous as undeserved success.

Most people who blame their luck
should question their judgement.

People are often called lucky when they go ahead and do
what others wish they'd done.

When one door closes, another opens,
but we often stare at the closed door so intently
that we don't see the one that opened.

The only sure thing about luck is that it will change.

Luck is opportunity meeting preparation.

A lot of what is *going* to happen
is being determined by what *is* happening.

Don't expect your ship to come in
if you haven't launched one.

You never know who you may meet
in the next five minutes.

Luck is usually against the person who depends on it.

Thank Lady Luck, but don't depend on her.

It takes a lot of luck
to make up for a lack of common sense.

Luck may get you a job but it won't let you keep it.

There's a silent "p" in luck.

Luck often comes disguised as hard work.

You are the genie — now go and find your lamp.

Someone else may deal the cards,
but how we play them is entirely up to us.

Marriage

I WAS PROBABLY TEN OR ELEVEN when they were courting, and they often took me for drives on a Sunday afternoon. He would be driving and she would be sitting right next to him. I, of course, was in the back seat. A couple of years later, after they had gotten married, I was again along on a Sunday afternoon drive. He was driving, but she was now seated almost against the passenger side door. I was still in the back seat. She said, "Before we were married, we always sat close to each other." He replied, "I'm sitting in the same place."

Success in marriage depends not so much on finding the right person as it does on being the right person.

The most important thing a father can do for his children is to love their mother.

When a married couple walks down the street, the one a few steps ahead is the one who's angry.

Walking ten blocks with a nagging spouse is more tiring than walking ten miles with an adoring sweetheart.

Meetings and Committees

THERE WERE SEVEN OR EIGHT OF US at the early morning meeting and Bob fell asleep. The rest of us crept out and another chap and I went down to the street and recruited six perfect strangers for this one. They sat around the table for a few minutes (the rest of us were watching from an adjoining room) and one of them made enough noise to awaken Bob. At that point another of them said, "Okay, Bob, we'll do it your way, but you'll have to shoulder the consequences if it doesn't work." Whereupon the six strangers got up and left. So did we. I think Bob sat there for a good half hour before he finally left. He never mentioned the incident to any of us.

A decision is what you have to make
when you can't find people to serve on a committee.

To kill an idea, refer it to a committee.

When a new idea comes up at a meeting,
insist upon hearing two positive points about it
before any negative comments are allowed.

Meetings are where people talk about things
they should be doing.

Whenever one person can adequately do a job,
two people can never do it as well, and it likely won't get
done at all if three or more people get involved.

When a mosquito lands on you,
don't form a committee, just kill it.

A committee of five usually consists of
one who does the work, three who praise him,
and one who writes a minority report.

Even smart people make dumb committees.

Sometimes taking minutes wastes hours.

Meetings, speeches and books
should never be judged by their length.

Mistakes

I SUPPOSE WE MAY KNOW why we make some mistakes, but for the most part a mistake is just that — a mistake. And we don't know why we made it. My co-worker, the Bopper, had made a mistake that caused an important shipment to end up in St. John's, Newfoundland, rather than Saint John, New Brunswick. This was when we were working for the railroad (he still does, incidentally) and occurrences like this required a form to be filled out. One of the questions that had to be answered was: "Why did you make this error?" Bopper told the supervisor who was waiting for the form to be completed that he didn't know. The supervisor, who couldn't stand the Bopper at the best of times, snarled back, "Well, *I* know why you made the mistake." "Okay," said the Bopper, handing him the form, "then you fill it in."

People who never make mistakes
end up working for people who do.

Dumb questions are more easily handled
than dumb mistakes.

Reason makes mistakes, but conscience doesn't.

It's a mistake to be afraid to make a mistake.

If the possible gain far outweighs the potential loss,
it's a mistake *not* to try.

It'd be easier to learn from our mistakes
if we weren't so busy denying we made them.

Learn by others' mistakes.
We don't have time to make them all ourselves.

The way to handle a mistake is to be big enough to admit
it, wise enough to learn from it, and smart enough to fix it.

We're always going to make another mistake;
just make sure it's a new one.

Admitting to a mistake is just another way of saying
you're smarter now than you used to be.

People rarely make mistakes on purpose.

You can only stumble if you're moving.

Making a mistake isn't as important as what you do next.

When doing something stupid,
the degree of stupidity is usually in direct proportion
to the number of people watching.

The world is changing so fast
you couldn't be wrong all the time even if you tried.

Immortality can be assured by one monumental error.

Don't mind people thinking you're stupid,
but don't give them any proof.

Once you get a mouthful of scalding hot coffee,
whatever you do next is going to be wrong.

We can be more successful by admitting we're wrong
than by proving we're right.

Money

THE PROBLEM WITH BASING YOUR SELF-WORTH on money is that when you are with people who have more than you, you tend to feel inferior: and when you're with people who have less than you, you tend to feel superior. Neither is necessarily so.

When a person says money can do anything,
that's the first clue that he doesn't have any.

Money is a poor master but an excellent servant.

The most misquoted phrase from the Bible is:
"Money is the root of all evil." The real quotation is:
"The _love_ of money is the root of all evil."

If you think money is your only hope for security,
you'll never have security.
Real security comes from knowledge, skill and attitude.

It's nice to acquire the things money can buy,
but it's better not to lose the things that money *can't* buy.

Never talk about money with people who have a whole lot
more or a whole lot less than you do.

How much money you make
isn't as important as how much you keep.

One way to become rich is to convince people
it's in *their* interests for you to do so.

Spend what's left after saving
rather than saving what's left after spending.

Health is the only real wealth.

Don't halt the ceremony to pick up a penny.

If you've got money to burn,
you'll have no trouble finding someone with matches.

The price that must be paid for anything really worthwhile
is not money; it's work, love and self-sacrifice.

When prosperity comes, don't use it all at once.

Misers aren't much fun to live with,
but they make wonderful ancestors.

Even when they're broke,
some people have more money than brains.

Sometimes you pay the most for things you get for nothing.

Rich people have to find out how poor people live;
and poor people have to learn how hard rich people work.

Don't pay too high a price for money.

If every country is in debt, who's got the money?

You don't see hearses pulling U-Hauls.

I've never been poor, only broke.
Being poor is a state of mind.

It's easy to have principles when you're well off.
It's tougher to have them when you're poor.

Even rich people cry, and eventually die.

When you get something for nothing,
someone else gets nothing for something.

Turning off the light at the end of the tunnel
is a poor cost-cutting device.

A fool and his money
were lucky to get together in the first place.

Motivation

Mabel O'Brien was a country schoolteacher. Other than her friends, relatives and former students, probably no one would recognize her name. Yet, she was one of the greatest teachers of all time. Just ask any of her former students. Why can we say this with such certainty? Easily.

Because she made us *want* to learn, not because she intimidated us, but because she inspired us.

Satisfied needs don't motivate.

People do things for *their* reasons, not yours.

If *you* don't lead your life, someone will lead it for you.

Find something bigger than yourself to believe in.

Work harder to be respected than to be loved.

Better results are achieved by praising strengths
than by criticizing weaknesses.

Some opposition can help; kites rise against the wind,
not with it.

Praise loudly; blame quietly.

Leaders tailor motivation to individual needs.

There are two ways to get to the top of an oak tree —
climb it, or sit on an acorn and wait.

Negotiation

I LOVE NEGOTIATING, but I guess I had taken it too far this time. Chuck, my counterpart, jumped up, slammed his fist on the table and shouted, "You have every characteristic of a dog!" And then, after a short pause, added, "Except loyalty!"

Take tough steps only when
they are *guaranteed* to be advantageous.

Recognized tactics aren't tactics.

When preparing to negotiate with someone, spend three
times as much time thinking about what he is apt to say
than on thinking about what you're going to say.

Successful negotiation comes not from holding good
cards, but from the skilful playing of them.

Negotiate only with decision makers.

Know all there is to know about all the facts.
There is usually some specific information
that can make or break you.

Before risking anything,
be sure the potential benefits are worth the possible cost.

To successfully negotiate with anyone,
in any set of circumstances, you must determine their
needs and then fulfil at least some of them.

The main point in using leverage is not to overuse it.

Homework makes the difference in any negotiation.
Properly prepared negotiators
are already ahead of the game.

An important part of any negotiation
is knowing when to stop.

When negotiating with an intimidating person, imagine
him sitting there in a stupid looking pair of boxer shorts.

What's unprofitable to the other side
will eventually be unprofitable to you.

Accept what you believe to be true,
even if it hurts your case.

By giving up something of a lesser value,
you will sometimes achieve something of a higher value.

It's as important to know when to give up an advantage
as it is to know when to seize one.

Shift the focus from defeating each other
to solving the problem.

The needs of both sides are seldom the same.
So, it should be possible for both to "win" a negotiation.

Discuss one thing at a time.

Don't start negotiating
until you *completely* understand *all* the issues.

Don't let the other side set the tone.
Discuss the issues your way
and stay with your line of reasoning.

Only an idiot holds out for absolutely everything.

The biggest step you can take
is to meet the other person halfway.

Whether an ultimatum will work depends on the other
side's investment of time, money and effort. It also must
come at the end of a negotiation, *never* at the beginning.

Admitting that we don't have all the answers usually
results in the other side being more receptive.

Never belittle the other side.

A compromise is when both sides
get what neither of them wanted.

The best solution to any conflict
is one that helps both sides.

When both sides respect each other, disagreement can
remain a genuine effort to understand differences.

It's more important to determine *what* is right
than *who* is right.

When rejecting another person's idea,
reject only the idea, not the person.

Let the logic of the situation dictate the next move.

When a deal-breaker is introduced early in the negotiation, discuss it, but delay resolving it.

Don't relieve the other side's stress until you get something in return.

Never reveal your real deadline until you absolutely have to.

It's rare to be able to obtain the best outcome quickly. Quick means risk.

Silence can be a powerful tool. The other side is usually uncomfortable with your silence and may reveal some things they wouldn't have otherwise; also, silence is pretty hard to rebut.

Don't bother murdering someone who's already committing suicide.

Total win or total loss provides no options.

Tailor your argument to the personalities of those you are talking to; put it in their terms.

Prove your points with facts.
Generalizations are never as effective as specifics.

Before trying to persuade people,
put yourself in their shoes and try to anticipate
the objections they'll come up with.

You can't antagonize and persuade at the same time.

Open-mindedness

DAVE, THE MOST OPEN-MINDED PERSON I KNOW, and I were disagreeing at the executive committee meeting. "We're not that far apart," he said.

"Dave," I replied, "we are diametrically opposed!"

"Well," he suggested, "that's not that far apart."

Minds, like parachutes, function only when open.

An open mind is a very good thing;
but don't keep it so open that your brains fall out.

When we get too broadminded,
our thinking tends to get shallow.

Some open minds should be closed for repairs.

A deaf ear is the first symptom of a closed mind.

Few things die quicker than a new idea in a closed mind.

The narrower the mind, the broader the statement.

Open-minded people, realizing that there's
probably a better way to do everything,
welcome criticism without taking it personally.

People who won't consider the facts because they've
already made up their minds will never be leaders.

Opportunity

Ed, who had recently moved to Toronto from Winnipeg, asked me what the population of Toronto was. I told him (as it was at the time) about two million. "Good," he smiled, "I only have to get fifty cents from each one of them."

Always look for the opportunity.

No matter how negative a situation, it's bound to offer at least one opportunity that wasn't there before.

It's better to be ready without an opportunity than to have an opportunity when you're not ready.

Opportunities are never lost.
The ones we miss are taken advantage of by others.

The reason some people don't recognize opportunity
is because it's often disguised as work.

Opportunities are often disguised as problems.

When you kill time, you bury opportunity.

Intelligent people know problems are opportunities
to show what they can do.

Optimism / Pessimism

UPON SEEING GOLIATH, the Israelites thought, "He's so big, we can't hurt him."

But David thought, "He's so big, I can't miss him."

An optimist is a person who knows how sad the world
can be. The pessimist is forever finding out.

An optimist sees an opportunity in every calamity;
a pessimist sees a calamity in every opportunity.

Pessimists may turn out to be right;
but optimists have a lot more fun.

There's no point being pessimistic. It doesn't work.

A pessimist, upon smelling flowers,
looks around for the coffin.

Expect the worst and you'll probably get it.

Whether your glass is half full or half empty
depends on whether you're pouring or drinking.

Patience

I'M NOT GENERALLY REGARDED as a particularly patient person, but I do believe that patience may once have saved my life. In the summer of 1966, I was driving to Prince Edward Island for my annual vacation. Any delay on that trip might eventually mean missing a ferry, thereby adding hours to the journey. I pulled into a gas station in a little town about 100 kilometres east of Quebec City. The attendant told me he had to move a couple of cars before he could serve me. Normally, because I still had a quarter of a tank, I would have left and pulled into the next station. But, this day, for some reason, I waited patiently. The delay was about five minutes. A few miles down the road I came upon a multi-vehicle accident in which six people were killed and six seriously injured. I learned later the accident had happened about five minutes before I arrived on the scene.

A shortcut may lead to somewhere you weren't going.

Patience succeeds more than hurry. We get the chicken
by waiting for the egg to hatch, not by breaking it.

Look more carefully the second time into something that
you were certain of the first time.

A moment of patience may avert disaster;
a moment of impatience may ruin a life.

Patience is not a long race. It's a series of short races.

Patience is a blend of wisdom and self-control.

Waiting is often very difficult;
but it's often very worthwhile.

Patience is doing something else in the meantime.

Patience can be a bitter seed, but it produces sweet fruit.

It's not a very good idea to pull up a flower by its roots
to see how it's doing.

Impatience can be a greater liability than inexperience.

Patience is hiding your impatience.

It's easier to avoid your first temptation
than to satisfy all that follow.

Always distinguish between necessary haste
and impatience.

If you find yourself rushing too much,
consider what would happen if you took your time.

Be patient, rational and never impulsive.
But when your favourable moment arrives, seize it.

Never risk something because of pride or impatience.

Patience always pays dividends.

A cake can't be iced until it is baked.

The person who can't wait for retirement
is often the same one who can't figure out
what to do on a Saturday afternoon.

Beware the fury of a patient man.

Patience in a moment of anger may avoid days of sorrow.

Performance

HE WAS DR. JEKYLL AND MR. HYDE. You never knew what sort of performance to expect from him. He'd be a perfectly charming speaker before one audience, and then the next time turn into an insufferable, arrogant jerk. This inconsistency was holding him back in his career. He had a large family, I think about six kids — all pretty young at this stage of his career. Finally, one day I said to him as we were going into an important meeting, "Perform as if your kids were in the audience."

———————

The three basic types of people are those who make things happen, those who watch things happen, and those who wonder what happened.

Motion isn't always action.

When all is said and done,
there's usually more said than done.

Do what you can, with what you have,
wherever you happen to be.

Getting things done isn't always the same as doing things.

Some people think they can move mountains
provided someone else clears away the foothills.

Putting a limit on what you *will* do,
puts a limit on what you *can* do.

Initiative is doing the right thing without being told.

Doing two things at once is doing neither.

The old carpenter measures twice and saws once.

Sugar doesn't make the tea sweet — it's the stirring.

Becoming number one is easier than staying number one.

When the going gets tough, the tough get going.

Use what talents you have. The woods would be a quiet
place if no birds sang but those that sang best.

No one would have blamed Columbus for turning back,
but no one would have remembered him, either.

The best performance of today's duties
is the best preparation for the future.

Looking is one thing, seeing is something else.

Times become trying for those who aren't trying.

Long-term, consistent effort pays off in anything.

You'll astound everyone, including yourself,
if you do what you're capable of.

Ask yourself what you want to be,
then do what you have to do.

Between the big things we can't do and the little things we
won't do, lies the danger of doing nothing.

You can't build a reputation on what you are *going* to do.

Give a man a fish and he'll eat for a day.
Teach him how to fish and he'll eat for the rest of his life.

Be like a postage stamp.
Stick to one thing until you get there.

There's a difference between activity and accomplishment.

The secret of a green thumb is usually brown knees.

See it as it is and do it as it should be done.

Do what should be done
without waiting for someone to tell you to.

Do everything that's necessary to produce the results.

Keep your eyes on results, not methods.

Expand capabilities and choices.

If you're being run out of town,
get out in front and pretend you're leading a parade.

If it's uphill you're on the right track.

Don't wait for someone to bring you flowers —
plant a garden.

The difference between ordinary and extraordinary
is the little "extra."

What one thing, if you did it well,
would have a positive effect on your personal life?
Is there another one in your professional life?
Why aren't you doing them?

The only way to accurately predict the future
is to create it.

The problem with doing something halfway
is that the other half may be more important.

An archer hits his target, partly by pulling,
partly by letting go.

To get anywhere you have to start from where you are.

If you're going nowhere, and don't do something about it,
you'll get there.

If you can conceive it and believe it you can achieve it.

The person who risks nothing, does nothing, has nothing,
is nothing and stays nothing.

Put your best foot forward, and don't drag the other one.

If you have no competitive advantage—don't compete.

Results are what count.

If you can't improve your performance,
lower your demands.

Everybody is capable of doing more
than they think they can.

The closest some people ever come
to reaching their potential is when writing a résumé.

If you're shut out, don't peek through the keyhole.
Either kick the door down or go away.

It's easier to jump ahead from a springboard
than from a sofa.

If you're rowing the boat,
you usually don't have time to rock it.

Troupers troop and troopers troupe.

The person who thinks it can't be done
shouldn't interrupt the person doing it.

You can't improve if you give up too soon.

What you don't have as inspiration,
you have to get by perspiration.

We can't always get what we *want*,
but striving for it can get us what we *need*.

By avoiding doing something right,
we increase the odds of doing something wrong.

Only a mediocre person is always at his best.

Personality

WE WERE PARTNERS, but our personalities couldn't have been more different. One day, after a rather protracted argument, he said to me, "You know, Lyman, I wish you were a little more like me and I was a little more like you."

"I don't," I replied, "because if that was the case neither of us would probably be worth a damn."

Don't let loyalty become fanaticism,
caution become timidity, confidence become arrogance,
conviction become stubbornness,
moderation become weakness,
or humility become servility.

Personality is the total effect we have on others.

Personality is to a person what perfume is to a flower.

Personality is something you have
until you start depending on it.

Being cold, aloof or ill-tempered
will always be inconsistent with being liked.

Everyone can give pleasure.
One by coming into a room, another by going out.

Any person who cares for only one thing,
whatever it is, is a dangerous person.

Mistrust those who think everything is good,
those who think everything is evil, and especially,
those who are indifferent to everything.

You don't find yourself — you create yourself.

People who are uncomfortable with who they are
make others uncomfortable, too.

To truly judge people, watch how they treat those
who can do them no good whatsoever.

Putting personality ahead of character
will work only in the very short run.

Places

It's likely that the two "places" most universally referred to are Heaven and Hell. When our son Alan was about twelve years old, we got into a discussion about Heaven and Hell, and what kind of places they probably were. Alan told me that he didn't know for sure what Heaven was, but that he knew what Hell was. He said, "Hell is knowing what Heaven is and not being able to go there."

A small town is where
there's no place to go where you shouldn't.

Some desks are just wastebaskets with drawers.

Home is a place that when you go there,
they have to let you in.

The outdoors is what I have to go through
to get from my house to my car.

It's fine to think globally, but we have to live locally.

Poise

DON WAS A PARTNER in the firm and I was still a lowly new recruit when, angry about some real or imagined slight, I went into his office and tossed a hard-backed file on his desk with much more force than I intended, sweeping every single item, including the paper he was working on, off his desk and into a pile on the floor. Don looked up and asked, "Is something wrong?"

To avoid jumping to a conclusion,
keep both feet on the ground.

Poise makes you a master of any situation.

Poise can be developed a little at a time.

Poise is developed by overcoming anger,
nervousness and talking without thinking.

How a person handles a situation can be more important
than the situation itself.

Poise in all things and at all times
is something very few people have.

We're all elegant in our element.

You can't be poised and angry at the same time.

Politics

IT'S A WELL-KNOWN FACT in our family that when Anne and I got married, in addition to the usual marriage vows, we made one extra to each other. I promised I'd never enter politics, and she promised she'd never get fat, a promise she's kept. A few years ago, as Anne cut herself a second piece of dessert, our son Alan turned to our other son, Matthew, and remarked, "I guess Dad can go into politics now."

Politicians talk about things they don't understand
and then try to convince us that it's our fault.

Politicians get votes from the poor and money from the
rich by promising to protect each from the other.

Politicians may make strange bedfellows, but they all
share the same bunk.

No politician is as worthy of praise
as the entrepreneur who creates wealth and employment.
Politicians tend to destroy both.

If God had been a Liberal, we'd have ten suggestions,
not commandments.

If politicians take credit for the rain
they should be prepared to accept blame for the drought.

The difference between a politician and a statesman
is that a politician worries about the next election
while a statesman worries about the next generation.

Politicians are like diapers. They should be changed often,
and for the same reason.

Politicians who do only what polls indicate people will
vote for are not leaders. Consensus following is not
leadership because by the time a consensus is reached
it's almost always too late to act.

All politics are local.

Pot Pourri

THE WAY THE ENGLISH LANGUAGE evolves is truly remarkable. The first meaning listed in my dictionary for the term
pot pourri is "a jar of flower petals and spices used for
scent." Yet, the literal translation from the original French
is "rotten pot." It's little wonder that the term has come to
mean any miscellaneous collection.

The reason I don't like to run is it makes me tired.

There are people with whom I share nothing
except the right to trial by jury.

No secret is safe with anyone else.

Don't step on anything soft.

Don't knock the weather; ninety percent of the population
couldn't start a conversation without it.

There's no reason to attack the monkey
if the organ grinder is there.

The more power is divided
the more irresponsible it becomes.

Little things can be very important,
what good is a bathtub without a plug?

If the grass is greener on the other side,
the water bill is probably higher too.

Laziness has produced a lot of great inventors.

It'd be nice to have more blessings that aren't in disguise.

It's okay not to be on the steamroller
as long as you don't become part of the road.

If the world were perfectly logical,
men would ride side-saddle, not women.

One thing you can do better than anyone else
is read your own writing.

Perhaps *who* you know is as important as *what* you know,
but it's also important who knows you.

My tailor takes new measurements every time I go to him,
but everybody else uses their old measurements of me.

I can advise a few rich clients, or a lot of poor clients —
but not both.

Anything left to run by itself can only go downhill.

A rose smells better than a cabbage,
but it doesn't make better soup.

Diets are for those who are thick and tired of it.

Never eat anything at one sitting that you can't lift.

Stop eating when you've had enough.
There's no need to keep going until you get tired.

Good people won't thrive in a bad environment.
Flowers have to be watered.

You have to be important to arouse jealousy.

On an anvil, it's better to be leather than granite.

Problems

DID YOU EVER NOTICE, when doing course assignments or tests, in a subject such as English or geography, it's "Question 1," "Question 2," and so on, but in math it's "*Problem* 1," "*Problem* 2," etc. I had enough trouble with math without this additional psychological hurdle, so I renamed them "Opportunity 1," "Opportunity 2," etc.

I rationalized this change as follows. If I knew the answer, it was an opportunity for me to strut my stuff. If I didn't know the answer, it was an opportunity for me to learn something.

Anticipation prevents problems.

One sure way to mishandle a problem is to avoid facing it.

The cost of solving a problem
is usually less than the cost of ignoring it.

If your problems were less difficult,
someone with less ability might have your job.

The first step in solving any problem is to begin.

I have more problems with Lyman MacInnis
than with any other person I know.

A problem well stated is a problem half solved.

It isn't always that people can't see a solution.
It's often that they can't see the problem.

A road with no potholes probably doesn't lead anywhere.

A new problem is sometimes as good as a day off.

Dealing with a tough problem can bring success —
as long as it's not a problem you've had before.

Problems are opportunities to succeed.

Real problems can be overcome;
only the imaginary ones can't.

If you haven't struggled for success
you can't fully appreciate it.

Ninety percent of the people who hear about our problems
don't care about them, and the other ten percent
are glad we have them.

The best way out of a problem is through it.

Problems are opportunities in work clothes.

If you don't have the will to overcome a problem,
you better have the wits to avoid it.

Don't quit just because the going gets rough,
but it won't hurt to pause to see if there's a better way.

Deal with adversity; don't report it.

When faced with a difficult situation
you have to alter it or you.

Got a problem? Take care of it.

Problems may cow the weak,
but the strong use them as instruments.

Don't use long-term solutions for short-term problems.

Deal with problems before they become crises.

When people are given the chance to open up without too many advice-giving interruptions, they often solve their own problems just by talking them through.

You have to believe that problems can be solved.

The answer to "what should I do?"
is always "what needs to be done."

We may not be responsible for our problems,
but we are responsible for their solutions.

When faced with an obstacle,
instead of praying to have it removed
thank the Lord for the opportunity to overcome it.

Procrastination

HE NEEDED TO BE DISCIPLINED for making a mistake that caused a serious problem with a client of the firm, but as it was Friday afternoon I decided to put it off until Monday rather than perhaps spoil his weekend. Although I can't honestly say the unfinished business spoiled *my* weekend, it did enter my mind from time to time. At the close of our conversation on Monday, I asked him if he had any comments. "Just one," he said, "I wish you had done this on Friday. I knew you'd have to deal with this in some way and I couldn't relax at all this weekend wondering what the effect would be. Now I can get on with my work."

Nothing is as exhausting as an unfinished task.

The best preparation for tomorrow is doing,
to the best of your ability, *today's* work today.

Do you realize how tiring it is to stand still?

It's easy not to be able to find time
to do the things we don't want to do.

The only thing you can be absolutely sure of accomplishing
is what you do right now.

When we coast we can only go downhill.

If something unpleasant needs to be done, do it now.

People who accomplish the most
are those who don't wait to be in the mood.
When something needs to be done, they do it.

The future is when we'll wish we'd done
what we aren't doing now.

The quickest solution is to do it.

People who wait until they feel like doing something
rarely do.

We are consistently outperformed
by the person who does today
what the rest of us were thinking about doing tomorrow.

Hard work is often the result of easy tasks not done.

You can't do *everything* at once,
but you can do *something* at once.

We are judged by what we finish, not by what we start.

Planning is good, but too much planning
may be just an excuse for not doing anything.

You can't build a reputation on what you were going to do.

It's amazing how many things we have to do,
and yet how important it is that we do them.

Successful people do the best they can with conditions as
they are. They don't wait for things to get better.

He who considers too much will perform too little.

By all means take time to think.
But when action becomes absolutely necessary, act.

Be sure tomorrow isn't the busiest day of the week.

The time to do what you have to do
is when it should be done.

Do it. Do it right. Do it right now.

Don't be the kind of person who's always getting ready
for the last thing that happened.

Tomorrow usually gets here before we're ready for it.

You never know how soon it will be too late.

Today was tomorrow yesterday.

Dig the well before you get thirsty.

Few things establish confidence
as quickly as doing things on time and as promised.

Many of us spend half our time wishing for things we
could have if we didn't spend half our time wishing.

Don't let what you need to do
get to you before you get to it.

Professionalism

No matter how smart, educated or skilful a person may be, it's the willingness to do a little extra that makes the difference between an amateur and a professional. Professionals do what's expected of them, and then some. It's hockey players like Wayne Gretzky, Gordie Howe and Bobby Orr who would stay out on the ice for extra practice, not fringe players whose names we can't remember. It's entertainers like Anne Murray who rehearse the extra hours. It's the medical specialist who devotes extra time to keeping up to date who's most in demand.

Professionalism can't be inherited or bequeathed;
it's a personal thing acquired through knowledge,
skill and dedication of purpose.

Professionals never have to fake it.

A professional comes back to work
regardless of what happened the day before.

The willingness to try again
separates the pro from the amateur.

It doesn't pay to be an amateur.

No matter how smart, educated or skilful a person may
be, it's the willingness to do a little extra that makes the
difference between an amateur and a professional.
Professionals do what's expected of them, and then some.

Hucksters are interested in their own personal gain,
professionals are interested in serving their clients.

Professionals perform well even when
they don't feel like it. Amateurs have trouble doing their
job even when they do feel like it.

Professionals do their best when it matters most.

It's easy to tell when a professional's attention wanders —
he makes a mistake.

Doing something right once doesn't make you a pro.

Learning to do anything well takes time and effort.

Amateurs hope. Professionals work.

Only amateurs stay angry; pros get over it.

Professionals are usually the ones who practise the most.

Promises

I THINK A PROMISSORY NOTE (a written promise to pay a sum of money) is the perfect embodiment of what all promises should be. With a promissory note, the person to whom the promise has been made has tangible evidence that can be presented to the promisor. When we make any promise, we should act as if the other person has such a piece of paper evidencing it.

Then we should redeem that imaginary piece of paper as soon as possible.

———————————

People who deliver more than they promise win respect; those who promise more than they deliver lose it.

The slowest in making a promise
may be the most faithful in keeping it.

Performance has much more value than promises.

A courteous "no" is always better than a broken promise.

Honour every promise, but don't make too many.

Don't make promises on another's behalf.
Promise only what you can deliver yourself.

Public Speaking

I KNOW THREE THINGS FOR SURE about public speaking. First, it is the most universally feared activity on the face of the earth. Second, it is not an art; it is a skill that can be learned, just like skating, swimming or riding a bicycle. Third, you can't learn it without doing it.

A speech is like a love affair. Anyone can start one, but it takes skill to properly end one.

If you don't strike oil in the first three minutes, stop boring!

A one-minute anecdote is worth an hour of history.

The unforgivable sin in public speaking is to forget about the audience.

Everyone is eloquent speaking about what they know well.

To explain something in clear and simple language,
you have to understand it yourself.

When trying to convince,
it's more important to stir emotion than thought.

Nothing can be said after forty minutes
that amounts to anything.

Speeches are like babies — easy to conceive
but very hard to deliver.

One specific is worth a thousand generalities.

Intellectuals use more words than necessary
to tell more than they know.

If your audience doesn't understand you, you're failing.

When choosing between two words,
always use the one that's easier to understand.

Just because you're familiar with an example
doesn't mean your audience is.

Use graphs to illustrate *relative* values;
tables for *specific* values.

When you are speaking, you're the leader.

When you're speaking, be sure they can see your heart
as well as your face.

Always include shortening in your recipe for a speech.

Public speaking is a lot like spelling "banana."
You have to know when to stop.

Laughter is better than applause because people applaud
to be polite. But laughter is a genuine response.

If you don't speak effectively,
people can't help you get what you want.

People who feel it strongly can say it well.

Facts inform but passion persuades.

Punctuality

THINK FOR A MOMENT about the signals you send by being late. You're telling other people that:

   a) You are more important than they are.
   b) The things you have to do are more important than the things they have to do.
   c) You're not very well organized.
   d) You're irresponsible.
   e) You're insensitive to their feelings.
   f) All of the above.

People recall all the faults
of those who keep them waiting.

When people are kept waiting
they will always be less pleasant to deal with.

Being late is an insult to everyone else involved.

Quality

WHEN WE BUY SOMETHING CHEAP, we're happy when we pay for it and disappointed every time we use it. When we buy a quality article, we may be a little unhappy when paying for it, but we'll be pleased every time we use it.

Quality is never an accident.

Do your best and the best will come back to you.

People will forget how fast you did a job,
but they'll remember how well you did it.

Half right is also half wrong.

The quality of a person's life is usually in direct proportion to their commitment to excellence.

Whatever you are, be a good one.

Refuse to accept anything but the best
and you'll get it more often.

When you're average,
you're as close to the bottom as to the top.

Do your best and things will turn out right.

Whatever you do, dignify it with your best.

How much we do is important,
but how well we do it is critical.

Deal only with people in whom you have confidence.

A great source of quality is pride in what you're doing.
Being good at it is fine, but being proud of it is essential.

Seeking perfection is frustrating;
seeking excellence is gratifying.

You can't have a quality product or service
if you hire cheap people.

Quantity is what you count. Quality is what you count on.

Good enough is the enemy of best.

It's harder to keep a first-class person in a second-class job than it is to keep a second-class person in a first-class job.

Regrets

WE'VE ALL HAD, have, and will have, regrets. People who say "I have no regrets" are really saying they've learned how to deal with their regrets. And there *are* specific ways to deal with a regret. If an apology is required, then apologize. If something needs to be done or undone, and it's possible to do so, then do or undo it. If none of the foregoing applies, forget it. Learn from it, then forget it.

Yesterday can't be changed. You can only make the most of today and prepare for tomorrow.

Look back only to learn, and look ahead only to plan.

Today's regrets limit tomorrow's possibilities.

The degree of regret usually depends on
the amount of attention you give it.

Rather than just regret it; do something about it.

No one likes to be around depressed people. So don't be.

Cancel the next pity party
you're going to throw for yourself.

If you quarrel with the past you may lose the future.

Accept the occasional disappointment as part of life
and continue to make the best of it.

Relaxation

THERE'S A TIME AND PLACE to relax. And sometimes being relaxed is a danger signal. I've taught public speaking for over forty years, and when people tell me they are relaxed before giving a talk, I tell them not to give it. If you're relaxed before giving a speech, it doesn't mean you're a pro. It means you don't care enough about your topic, your audience, or both. On the other hand, if you ever fall asleep in the dentist's chair without the benefit of anaesthetic, please let me know your secret.

Nothing adds more to the pleasure of relaxation
than doing things when they are supposed to be done.

The best time to relax
is when you don't have the time for it.

What we do with our leisure time is almost as important
to our success as what we do during our working hours.

You can't truly enjoy doing nothing
unless you have a lot of things that need to be done.

Revenge

TRYING TO GET REVENGE is about the most useless and counter-productive activity I can imagine. And of all the types of revenge I've seen attempted over the years, the most ridiculous is that of the person who sells a stock because they're mad at it. The stock doesn't know you bought it.

You can't get ahead of someone by getting even with him.

Taking time to suck out the venom
is more productive than chasing the snake.

Revenge is like biting a dog because he bit you.

Nobody will ever get ahead of you
while kicking you in the seat of the pants.

To cure a hurt, forget it.

Hating someone is like burning down your house
to get rid of a rat.

While you're nursing your grudge, they're out dancing.

You can't hold a person down
without staying down yourself.

Today's enemy may be tomorrow's ally.

Rudeness

WHY IS IT THAT PEOPLE who would never put me on hold for twenty minutes if I called them on the telephone, will keep me waiting for twenty minutes in their reception area?

***

When you're rude you're telling people they don't matter;
when you're nice you're telling them they do.

Profanity makes you very popular —
with about one percent of the human race.

What you do to others, you do to yourself.

Jumping into a muddy puddle makes it muddier.

Remind rude salespeople that they're overhead,
you're profit.

You don't *have* to take insults personally.

Never act or speak when driven by jealousy or resentment.

Where there is shouting, there is no true communication.

The next time you're about to humiliate someone,
remember the last time you were humiliated.

Vulgar people delight in the faults of the great.

Rudeness is an ineffective person's imitation of power.

Rudeness is a weak person's imitation of strength.

A civil "no" is always better than a rude "yes."

Beating others at politeness is a great victory.

No one is too big to be courteous, but many are too small.

Courtesy makes a better trap than rudeness.

Support *your* beliefs, don't ridicule other people's.

Sweet words are always easier to swallow.

Self-confidence

WHEN I WAS IN MY MIDDLE TEENS, I developed a stutter. By
the time I was eighteen, I had trouble pronouncing my
own name. This was particularly bothersome because I
wanted to be a radio announcer. My former schoolteacher,
Mabel O'Brien, suggested I take the Dale Carnegie
Course. After five sessions of this remarkable training my
stutter disappeared and, as of this writing at least, has not
returned. A miracle? Not really. The course simply gave
me enough self-confidence.

Self-confidence is the first requirement of success.

Self-confidence, in itself, is of no value;
it has to be utilized.

The greatest sources of confidence are the ability to do something well and a complete knowledge of a subject.

Look confident and it's easier to *be* confident.

Confidence is not just feeling secure;
it's also being able to tolerate insecurity.

Self-confidence and honesty
are an unbeatable combination.

Don't hesitate to go out on a limb — it's where the fruit is.

Confidence is entering a contest
and wondering who's going to finish second.

Confidence allows you to feel right about something
without having to prove someone else is wrong.

The most confident person at a meeting
is the one who's done his homework.

Overconfidence is that cocky feeling you get
just before you know better.

Next to success,
knowledge is the greatest confidence builder there is.

Self-confidence allows you to be comfortable with people who aren't like you.

People who have no confidence in themselves rarely have confidence in others.

Selling

THERE ARE AS MANY THEORIES about selling as there are salesmen, ranging all the way from incompetents like Willy Loman to some of the super salesmen TV evangelists. The best selling job I ever witnessed was the sale of a brand new 1958 Pontiac to a farming couple in rural Saskatchewan, neither of whom could drive. This wasn't really an offensive act because the couple could clearly afford the car, and I thought at least one of them would learn to drive. Five years later the car still sat, unused, in their granary. When I asked the salesman how he ever managed to make that sale, he told me he convinced the couple that they shouldn't sit by and have their hated neighbour be the first in the area to have that year's model.

An effective sales presentation has a good beginning and a good ending, both of which are as close together as possible.

You'll never close the sale
if you aren't talking to the right person.

People don't buy something for many reasons.
They usually buy it for *one* reason
that happens to be the most important to them.

It's hard to sell something you wouldn't buy yourself.

Forget about sales you hope to make
and concentrate on the service you want to render.

People must buy *you*
before they will buy what you're selling.

The most important thing is not what a salesperson
says — it's what the buyer believes.

In selling, it isn't enough to aim to please;
you must constantly improve your marksmanship.

The potential business from any sales effort
has to be enough to justify your time and effort.

If you can't make a sale, at least make a good impression.

People don't buy products and services —
they buy the satisfaction of using them.

Give your customers a little more than they pay for,
and they'll always come back.

Sell your product or service on value, not price.

Ask what would happen if the customer did nothing
about his "problem." This will usually increase
his sense of urgency.

Use the language that your customer uses. But don't use
his buzz words unless you've earned the right to.

A successful product must have an easily perceived value.

Anybody working for a commission is going to earn every
dime he makes selling me something.

No matter how much people may *need* something,
they usually have to *want* it before they'll buy it.

You can't sell the coat until the customer tries it on.

The objective of the salesperson is not to make sales.
It's to make customers.

A customer who constantly makes unreasonable demands
is not a customer worth keeping.

Know your competitors, but know your customers better.

Customer service isn't *somebody's* job; it's *everybody's* job.

Keeping a customer costs a mere fraction of the cost
of getting a new one.

Shout the advantage.

Know *their* business but know *your* stuff.

Customers never lose arguments.

Silence

THE OLD CHAP LIVED in a rundown shack right beside the railroad track. Every night at midnight a noisy freight train rumbled by, shaking the shack. Then, one night, after forty-three years, the train didn't come by. The old guy jumped out of bed and yelled, "What was that!"

Silence is never more golden than when held long enough
for you to get all the facts.

Speak only when you can improve on the silence.

When a person doesn't talk to you,
he's telling you something.

Silence is often mistaken for wisdom.

There's a time to speak and a time to remain silent.
Wisdom is knowing the difference.

Silence is often the *best* comment.
If something goes without saying, let it.

Most of us know how to say nothing.
The key is to know when.

When something you'd really like to say
can't possibly do any good, say nothing.

There's nothing wrong with having nothing to say,
unless you insist on saying it.

The art of conversation includes saying the right thing
at the right time, and *not* saying the wrong thing
at the wrong time.

Always say less than you think.

A sure way to keep people from jumping down your
throat is to keep your mouth shut.

"Nothing" is sometimes a good thing to do
and often a brilliant thing to say.

Everybody has a right to have opinions,
but not necessarily the right to express them.

What you don't say, you don't have to explain.

Silence is the only satisfactory substitute for intelligence.

Silence is the ultimate weapon of leadership.

You never have to explain what you don't say.

It's fine to let your mind go blank
as long as you also turn off the sound.

An ounce of *don't-say-it* is worth a ton of *I-didn't-mean-it*.

It's easier to swallow angry words now
than to eat them later.

You have not converted a person
because you have silenced him.

Smiles

TRY THIS LITTLE EXERCISE. For one whole day, smile at least once each time you're dealing with a person. Then, for one whole day, avoid smiling as much as possible. Compare how *you* felt at the end of each of these days, let alone how differently the people you were dealing with probably felt.

A smile is an outer reflection of an inner condition.

A smile always adds to your face value.

Of all the things we wear,
our expression is the most important.

When you feel good, let your face know.

You can be as decisive with a smile on your face
as you can with a scowl.

Everyone smiles in the same language.

If you have to do it anyway,
you may as well do it with a smile.

Socialism

THE WEAK CAN'T BE STRENGTHENED by weakening the strong. Employees can't be helped by destroying employers. The poor can't be enriched by impoverishing the rich. Character can't be developed by destroying independence. People aren't helped by doing for them what they could do themselves. Socialists think so, but history constantly proves them wrong.

The inherent vice of capitalism is the unequal sharing
of blessings; the inherent virtue of socialism
is the equal sharing of misery.

Pitting the poor against the rich will certainly make the
rich poor, but it won't make the poor rich.
If you doubt this, study the French Revolution.

Liberals and socialists should spend less time complaining about the distribution of income and more time thinking about how to create it.

There are only two places where socialism could work:
In Heaven, where it's not needed;
and in Hell, where they already have it.

If socialists don't learn that there should be a reward for winning and a penalty for losing, the whole framework on which our progress has been based will disappear.

Socialists want *their* conscience to be *your* guide.

Sports

SPORTS CAN TEACH MANY LESSONS. Let's consider just one of the hundreds it taught me. I was a hockey goaltender in organized leagues for about twenty-five years. Even if I had been the best goaltender the world has ever known, so good that I never allowed even one single goal to be scored on me, without the effort of my teammates I would never have won a single game!

The trouble with being a good sport
is that you have to lose to prove it.

To enjoy baseball you don't need violence in your heart.

To coach you have to be smart enough to understand the game and stupid enough to think it's important.

Winning isn't everything — but wanting to is.

Sport doesn't *create* character, it *reveals* it.

You can learn more about a person in half an hour of play
than in a year of socializing.

Golfers blame fate for landing in a sand trap,
but take full credit for a hole in one.

An early loss removes the pressure
of trying to remain undefeated.

Maybe we can't win, but we don't have to lose right away.

Winning is the state of affairs just before losing.
But the reverse is also true.

The will to win is worthless without the will to prepare.

A well-adjusted person is one who can play bridge and
golf as if they were games.

Some people are good losers. Others can't act.

Statistics

THREE STATISTICIANS were hunting deer. A beautiful, big buck appeared on the crest of the hill. The first statistician aimed, fired, and missed five feet to the left of the animal. The second statistician aimed, fired, and missed five feet to the right. The third jumped up and yelled, "We got him!"

Statistics show that the best time to buy anything
is about twenty-five years ago.

All other things being equal,
fat people use more soap than thin people.

Put your head in a furnace and your feet on a cake of ice
and on average you should feel pretty good.

Statistics, like expert witnesses, will testify for either side.

Statistics are no substitute for judgement.

Averages are made up of the really good times
and the really bad times.

When you come across something
that defies the law of averages, seek the reason.

Stubbornness

TWO MULES WERE TIED TOGETHER by a short rope. There was a bale of hay at each end of the field. The mules kept straining to reach the nearest bale of hay until they finally died of starvation. If even one mule had given in, they could have eaten first one bale of hay and then the other.

Stubbornness has the dubious advantage
of always knowing what you'll be thinking.

Being stubborn is okay if you're right about the thing
you're being stubborn about.

There are two types of people who never change their minds:
dead people and fools.

Don't confuse courage of conviction
with stubbornness of prejudice.

If you don't take the turn in the road,
it may become the end of the road.

Success

SUCCESS IS RARELY a single, self-contained unit. It's often a crowning event following a series of previous, but lesser, successes. For example, the baseball player on a World Series championship team probably had a career something like the following: star Little League player; high school batting champion; high draft pick; minor league home run leader; minor league player of the year; major league player; and, finally, the World Series. The many successes along the way may seem unimportant after the World Series win, but each one was just as big in its own time. And others will probably follow. About the only thing that can be said with certainty about success is that it's always personal.

For every person who climbs the ladder of success,
there are a dozen still waiting for the elevator.

To succeed you must be willing to fail.

Three stages of success: start, go, keep going.

To become a success, have fun doing what you do.

Success isn't out looking for you.

One way to succeed
is to do things that failures don't like to do.

Sometimes a very important ingredient of success
is a competent, tireless enemy.

Wisdom is knowing *what* to do;
skill is knowing *how* to do it; success is *doing* it.

One of the qualities of successful people in all walks of life
is keen observation.

The success of others has no bearing on your success.

Success depends not just on how well you do things
you like to do, but also on how well you do things
you *don't* like doing.

You're not a success
if you had to violate the rights of others.

Success isn't how far you got,
it's the distance you travelled.

Success is doing what you like to do
and making a living at it.

One way to succeed in life
is to act on the advice you give to others.

The really successful person can say "no"
without giving a reason.

Success is the reward
for taking enough time to do something well.

If at first you succeed, try something harder.

If you love your work you're a success.

Satisfaction is success.

Success is better measured
by the obstacles you've had to overcome
than by where you are.

To be really successful, continue to look for work
after you've found a job.

The difference between success and failure
is a bunch of little things.

Whenever you see success you know that somewhere
someone made a key decision.

Success: getting up when you fall down.

There are only two reasons for not getting what you want.
Either you don't want it badly enough
or you aren't prepared to pay the price.

Success is accomplishing something.

Success is knowing you have worked hard
and done your best.

Aim for achievement and success will follow.

There are enough different kinds of success
for everyone to have some.

The difference between a successful person
and a failure is often a simple lack of will.

Success sometimes comes from knowing the right questions to ask rather than knowing all the answers.

Successful people look for the circumstances they want, and if they can't find them, make them.

You can't just *let* things happen. You have to *make* things happen.

People who see needs and provide for them without being told will succeed.

Stability is more essential to success than brilliance.

You're more apt to achieve success by striving to deserve it than by striving to attain it.

Three ways to succeed: be first; be best; be different.

Success is more attitude than aptitude.

To succeed, be prepared to deal with pressure, tension and discipline.

Always remember what got you there.

Successful people aren't destined to succeed,
they're determined to.

To succeed, first find something you like to do so much
you'd do it for nothing; then learn to do it so well
that people will pay you for it.

The only place where success comes before work
is in the dictionary.

Time Management

THE ONLY CONSTANT in effective time management is that all of us have the same twenty-four hours available to us every day. That's the only given. There's no such thing as one person having more time than another. Once you accept the fact that we each have twenty-four hours a day, time management becomes an absolutely personal scenario.

We make time to do what we really want to do.

Do it, delegate it, or ditch it.

Never get so busy that you don't have time to think.

You take care of the days —
the calendar will take care of the years.

274

Don't waste your time thinking you can do other people's jobs better. Use it to improve your performance.

Time is usually wasted in minutes, not hours.
A bucket with a tiny hole in the bottom will get just as empty as one with a huge hole. It will just take longer.

Never let the fact that you can't do everything you want to do keep you from doing what you can do.

If you don't have time to do it right the first time, you'll never have time to do it over.

Days are like identical suitcases;
some can pack more into them than others.

Deadlines should be based on what you *can* do, not on what you'd *like to* do. You will often achieve more by having a number of shorter deadlines than by having one long one.

Changeable deadlines aren't deadlines.

It's ridiculous to complain that our days are too short if we act as if there'll be no end to them.

There's a limit to the things you can control,
so concentrate on those.

People who make the worst use of time are usually the
same ones who complain there's not enough of it.

The strongest memory is weaker than the palest ink,
so make notes.

If you're already really busy,
drop an old activity before adding a new one.

No one ever said on his deathbed,
"I wish I'd spent more time at the office."

If you have three hours to chop down a tree,
spend two sharpening your axe.

Monitor your activities.

Be sure you're doing what's important
rather than simply reacting to what seems urgent.

If you fill your day with time-sensitive activities,
you'll have no time left to deal with emergencies.

Be as wary of *not* doing the things you *want* to do,
as you are of *doing* the things you *don't* want to do.

Don't let obsessions conflict with responsibilities.

Do at least one thing every day
that you would rather put off until later.

Everything can't be a number one priority.

Even the best horse can't wear two saddles.

Things that matter most shouldn't be subject
to things that matter least.

When you kill time
you might be murdering an opportunity.

Be sure your diary has room
for uninterrupted thinking time.

Time is a valuable asset.
Each minute is a miracle that will never happen again.

Truth

IT'S AMAZING HOW OFTEN people start sentences with statements such as, "Well, to tell the truth ..." or, "To be perfectly honest ..." Does this mean that when they *don't* preface their remarks with such qualifications, they *aren't* telling the truth?

As scarce as truth is,
the supply still seems greater than the demand.

Truth is like surgery. It hurts, but it cures.

Stretch the truth and people will see through it.

Walk in, plant yourself, look the other person in the eye,
and tell the truth.

Truth and justice are necessary for society to endure.

The trouble with a half truth
is that you may get the wrong half.

Truth is also shorter than fiction.

Don't tamper with truth.

Wisdom

Wisdom manifests itself in many ways. The story is told about Cary Grant and some friends entering a posh New York restaurant without reservations. Upon being informed by the maitre d' that they would have a half-hour wait, one of them whispered to Cary, "Tell him who you are!" Cary replied, "If I have to *tell* him who I am, then I'm not."

The beginning of wisdom is knowing when to stop.

The best symbol of wisdom is a bridge.

Common sense in an uncommon degree is called wisdom.

The handwriting on the wall may be a forgery.

Believe only what you understand.

We'd lose half our wisdom if we lost our clichés.

Everyone is a fool a few times every day.
Wisdom consists of not exceeding the limit.

We can be knowledgeable with other people's knowledge,
but we can't be wise with other people's wisdom.

Wisdom includes knowing what to overlook.

Sometimes it's better to judge people
by what they'd like to be rather than what they are.

Knowledge can come from taking things apart,
but wisdom only by putting things together.

Whale wisdom: "When you're spouting, you're most likely
to be harpooned."

Hindsight is good; foresight is great; insight is best.

Logic sometimes has to take a back seat to understanding.

Being wise often consists simply in knowing
what to overlook.

The best way to get credit for an accomplishment
is to give it away.

Don't ignore a good suggestion
because you don't like the source.

Don't confuse an absence with a loss.

When two people agree on everything,
one of them is unnecessary.

A mentor's hindsight becomes the protégé's foresight.

No roots, no fruits.

One difference between wisdom and stupidity is that
wisdom has limits.

Don't ignore the voice in the wilderness—
it may be right.

Power is when people think you have power.

Even the sun burns if you get too much of it.

You can't pay cash for wisdom.
It's only available on the installment plan.

Work

QUALITY OF WORK is greatly affected by attitude. A young trucker, bored with his work, asked an older driver who always looked as if he was on a vacation what his secret was. The old driver said, "*You* went to work this morning, but *I* went for a drive in the country."

It's a mistake to think that we're working for someone else.

Nothing is work
unless you'd rather be doing something else.

If you don't like your work either change your attitude
or change your job.

In the right job, hard work is not work at all.

More people are fired for having a bad attitude
than for all other reasons combined.

If you love your job,
you'll never have to work a day in your life.

The most important part of your job
is to help your boss succeed.

Those who work just for the money rarely make as much
as those who also love their work.

The will to work hard may not be genius,
but it's the next best thing.

Easy jobs don't pay much.

There is no future in any job.
The future is in the person who does the job.

When people think their work doesn't matter,
quality deteriorates. But if a job wasn't important,
it wouldn't exist. All jobs aren't equal,
but they're all important.

The best investment anyone can make is hard work.

The best time to look for work is after you get a job.

If you do a good job you usually get to keep it.

Work done to the best of your ability
is one of life's most satisfying experiences.

Good work can be wasted by want of a little more.

Make your job important
and it will probably return the favour.

One way to get ahead
is to always make sure you're underpaid.

There are two kinds of people:
those who do the work and those who take the credit.
Be in the first group; there's less competition.

Rest and play are desserts, work is the main course.

What you receive for your work is sometimes not as
important as what you become because of it.

If we don't feel good about talking about what we do,
we should change our work.

There's a big difference between being tired and lazy.

Tasks we work hard at become easier.

When your work speaks for itself, don't interrupt.

Work is the link between wanting something
and getting it.

The person who got a good job probably did whatever
was necessary to do a good job.

Concentrate on the task at hand
and the promotion will come along.

If you can't be replaced, you can't be promoted.

If you can put your whole self into it,
it's not work — it's joy.

The best preparation for the future
is a job well done today.

Work is a verb not a noun.

Poor workers blame their tools.

Take your job seriously, but not yourself.

Believe in yourself and work hard.

Work to *become* something, not to *acquire* something.

An entrepreneur will work fifteen hours a day
to avoid working eight for someone else.

Easy street is a dead end.

The self-employed have the most demanding bosses.

What you have to work with isn't always as important
as how you work with what you have.
Shakespeare wrote with a feather, not a word processor.

Worry

I DOUBT THAT THERE IS A METHOD of overcoming worry that would work for everybody, but here's what works for me.

When I start worrying about something, it's almost always because I can't do anything about whatever it is that's worrying me; therefore, my worrying isn't very effective.

So, what I do is make an appointment to worry. I actually set aside a time, say fifteen minutes at 3:45 the next afternoon, during which I will worry really effectively. If I catch myself worrying about the subject before the appointed time, I remind myself to put if off. What usually happens is by 3:45 the next day rolls around, I've either forgotten the problem (do not write the "appointment" in your book) or something more important is occupying my thoughts. In the rare case where neither of the foregoing holds true, I'll worry as planned. But then my mind usually wanders after a few seconds, or I actually come up with a solution to the problem.

———————————

Concern is *fore*-thought, worry is *fear*-thought.

Don't read big implications into little facts.

Worry is the interest you pay on borrowing trouble.

You'll worry a lot less what people think of you
when you realize how seldom they do.

Don't worry about the future. If what you're worried
about doesn't happen, you worried needlessly.
If it does happen you'll worry twice.

Don't go mountain-climbing over molehills.

Take time to think, but not to tremble.

If you worry about what people think about you,
then you must have more confidence in their opinions
than in your own.

Worry is when your stomach is firing bullets
and your brain is firing blanks.

It's better to feel a little panic beforehand
and then be calm when things happen,
than to be calm beforehand
and panic when things happen.

We're in good shape when we're too busy to worry during
the day and too tired to worry at night.

Half the worry in the world is caused
by trying to make decisions before having enough
knowledge on which to base them.

Writing

IF READERS DON'T GET THE MESSAGE, you may as well not write it. Break long sentences into two or more short sentences, arranged in a logical order. Eliminate unnecessary adjectives and adverbs. Replace big words with conversational ones. Then you'll be understood.

Write not so that you may be understood
but so that you cannot be misunderstood.

Know the big words but use little ones.

The best writers give readers the most knowledge
in the least time.

Words, once written, have a life of their own.

In writing, the only person who really counts is the reader.

To write clearly, you must think clearly.